To

Lots of love [illegible]
beautiful family
[illegible] x

Where I belong...

Mary L Sibbit is a wife and mother of two children based in a small fishing town on the East coast of Scotland. From a very early age she knew she had a creative side and experienced life on a much deeper plane than the average person. She began to write down her thoughts and feelings as a form of therapy after finding it difficult to cope following tragic events in her life. By doing so she opened the door once more to her creative side after years of it being suppressed to concentrate on family life. Now she loves to write, paint, design and create and does so in a way to express her deep emotional feelings towards all of lives ups and downs.

Where I belong......

Mary L Sibbit

First published in Great Britain in 2015

ISBN: 978-1-329-43948-1

Printed in Great Britian by Lulu Printing Company

Also available as an eBook

For my husband – without you I am nothing
For my children – you are my life
For my parents – you mean the world to me
Without you all I would have nowhere to belong

This book has been written with both an act of power and of surrender. It may simply be the expression for women that they themselves, consciously or unconsciously at times had often thought or felt but were afraid to express. This is as honest an account of my life as I could possibly make it and has been written with a small sense of fear and a keen sense of what it may do. It has been written with my love and blessed with my soul. To protect some of the individuals, I have changed the places, names and some of their identifying characteristics to protect their privacy.

Acknowledgments

I am indebted to the following people for their help and support. To my husband Mark thank you for being there for me through out everything. Thank you for putting up with my madness and for supporting me and having my back though out all my crazy ideas. To my children thank you for being patient with me and for giving me the love that all mothers should feel. There is no love quite like it. To my parents, thank you for giving me the life I have today. Thank you for loving me and for giving me the basic skills in life that I needed to exist as I am today. And thank you to all my loyal friends and family who have supported me throughout this venture. Your encouragement holds a place in my heart.

Where I belong……

"Have you ever thought that if one thing hadn't happened, a whole set of things never would've either? Like dominoes, a single event kicked off and an unstoppable series of changes that gained momentum and spun out of control, and nothing was ever the same again. Don't ever doubt that a mere second can change your life forever. "

Prologue

I had always enjoyed sex, but didn't truly understand the power of it until I met my husband. I was only 14 when I lost my virginity. It was nothing like what I thought it would be and I just wasn't prepared for what would follow from opening that chapter in my life so early. I lived my teenage years thinking that sex would get me noticed not realising that it would do so in all the wrong ways. I longed to know where I belonged, a lost soul finding my place on this earth desperate to feel needed. The climax of my encounters with these guys was always a sham, even when they weren't too wrapped up in themselves to notice me. I was shy and guarded and never knew how to open up to people in all aspects of my life. I didn't know how to tell them what I wanted for fear of looking stupid. I had built a solid brick wall around myself and in doing so, became shielded by my fears.

I was lucky though as I encountered a special moment in my life that so many others can only dream off. A moment in time when a metamorphic thing happened and the cracks in my wall began to show, cracks that would eventually lead to the walls crumbling downfall, a downfall that allowed me to truly find myself. I was only nineteen when that special moment happened in my life. I had been touched by the soul of another human being right when I needed it most. I was feeling destined to follow a path of unhappiness when my husband first stepped into my life.

When someone touches your soul in such a way you get a feeling unlike any you have never encountered before. Your intuition kicks in and you just know that they are the one to save you from all the wrong in your life. He was my saviour. He was my.....Soul mate.

"I had a feeling that Pandora's box contained the mysteries of a women's sensuality, so different from a man's and for which man's language was so inadequate. The language of sex had yet to be invented. The language of the senses was yet to be explored" _*Anais Nin*

Chapter One

My earliest memories as a child were from around the age of three, when I lived in Dundee shortly before we moved up to Fort William. I don't remember the correct sequence of such memories but I do remember where they took place. We were living in Charleston, Dundee and I was just a toddler. I had somehow got my head trapped in the underside part of a dining room chair and my dad had had to come home from work to saw the chair apart to release my aching head. I remember my grandparents visiting from up north and sitting on my Grandpas knees and looking up at his handsome face and feeling loved. We had a blue budgie called Joey who would sit on my shoulder and bounce his head up and down and I loved to play on a large blow up animal possibly a turtle which was in the middle of our living room floor. I don't remember much else about that time in my life because most of my memories started from when we had moved up north to Fort William.

I must off been five years old when we had moved there as I had started school for the first time. I remember feeling lost and cold. I didn't want to be there in a place full of strangers. I hadn't gone to nursery so it was a huge leap going from home to school with a whole load of children that I didn't know. I can still remember the smell of my brown leather satchel school bag and the crinkling feeling of my crisps for playtime being tied up in a white wire twist tie as I couldn't yet open them myself. The school consisted of lots of different small buildings rather than one large building. The ceilings were tall or at least they seemed to be being so small. There was a small sandpit at the back of a double sided giant chalk board on wheels that we were allowed to play at after we finished our work. There was a series of tall paned windows in the room that over looked the loch across the main road from the school filling the room with white light. The gym hall which was in another building had huge brown, wooden entrance doors and had a big open space that echoed with the sound of our gym shoes squeaking on the polished wooden floors. I don't recall having any friends at school, possibly being why I remember it being such a cold and empty place.

Gran and Grandad Croll would sometimes travel up from Dundee to stay and I loved it when they did. I remember Gran buying me a She- Ra figure from a toy shop on the high street and playing with it as we trekked up the long steep hill to get home as we stayed on the ground floor of a multi story flat halfway up the hill side. I don't remember friends at school but I remember playing with children that stayed in the same block of flats and the one next to ours. Together we would paint by numbers and muck about in the entry close, pretending that the old woman at the top of the stairs was a wicked witch. They seemed to have lots of toys that I didn't and it was in their house that I first discovered Play-doh, falling in love with its smell. I had a very vivid imagination and would make up stories about Werewolves, telling my friends and cousins my make believe stories. There were dark damp patches on the walls outside our house after it had been raining and I would almost believe it myself that they were the markings of the wolves trying to get into the house at night when we were all sleeping.

Our kitchen had glass panes that opened the room out to the hallway and a table with two long benches at either side. I loved the cherry lollipops that my parents would buy. They came as a pair with green stems stored in a plastic tub in the kitchen pantry and I would devour them as a treat. We had two bathrooms side by side, one with the bath and the other with the toilet. Our living room had a huge window that overlooked the loch from a height and on windy days you could see the white crests of waves down bellow. We called them the white horses.

One night my Dad and Grandpa came home all excited and full of fun but I was confused as they both looked like they were covered in blood. It was years later that I learned that they had been extras in a new up and coming movie and the fake blood had been part of their costumes. It was from this memory that stemmed my fascination with the movie 'The Highlander', the Scottish scenery, the music, the lyrics, costumes, in fact everything about the movie. This movie with my family's link to it and the oil painting that hung on my Grans bedroom wall was why I fell in love with Eilean Donan Castle even though I had never visited it in person. I felt a strong gravitational pull towards the place from then right up to my present moment in time.

"You will enrich your life immeasurably if you approach it with a sense of wonder and discovery" *_Nate Berkus*

It was during our short stay in Fort William that I first discovered the sensations between my legs. My cousin had also discovered this and often we would talk about it and touch ourselves when no one was around. We were really close and would tell each other everything. It was exciting and fun, like a dirty little secret and we didn't want to get caught.

A few years later and now living back in Dundee, I discovered what it was like to have someone touch me. Only this was a dirtier secret. I was only about seven or eight at the time but both my best friend and I got close, a little too close. Both the same age and at the same school we had lots in common. A big group of us would hang around together, doing normal kids stuff, playing chase, climbing trees. But when we were alone things changed.

I remember a boy once flashing to us in his den and feeling excited. He wanted us to touch him but we were too scared so we watched him do it too himself instead. We each had boyfriends that we would kiss and laugh about afterwards like naughty little school girls. As best friends we got to know each other in a way that no other best friends usually do, especially at that age. We both knew about the tingling feelings between our legs when we applied pressure below but we decided to take it a step further, to do it to each other. We would use our hands, legs, anything we could think of to give us enough pressure and I loved it, the feeling it made, the rush and the fear of being caught. On one occasion we stripped completely naked and lay on top of one another grinding and sifting till we got the pressure we needed to let go, never any penetration just pressure. Penetration was something I wasn't aware of until secondary school.

I've never classed myself as a lesbian and never will but I suppose looking back, we felt comfortable with each other, felt close enough to share the discovery of the female orgasm. I just couldn't get enough of the feeling. The build up and crash as you hit the heights of pure pleasure. I would do it at every opportunity I could, while at school, under the table when everyone was too engrossed in their school work to notice, in bed at night all alone, out and about while riding on my bike. The slightest touch in that area and I wanted to peak. I had discovered a small part of myself and I just loved being me.

"Our parents deserve our honour and respect for giving us life itself. Beyond this they almost always made countless sacrifices as they cared for and nurtured us through infancy and childhood, provided us with the necessities of life and nursed us through physical illnesses and the emotional stresses of growing up" _Ezra Taft Benson

Chapter Two

I would say that I had a fairly good childhood. I loved the outdoors and was free to play and do almost as I wished. Not like it is nowadays. I was street wise and knew how to look after myself. Getting into fights wasn't something unusual but I could stand my ground, knew how to dig my nails in and rip the odd stand of hair out if I needed to. It's funny really as I'm nothing like it now, I hate confrontation. During the summer months I'd be out from dawn till dusk, called in only for dinner, tea and then bedtime. Always filthy, always a true sign of a happy child.

Where ever I was I'd be guaranteed to have my little brother not far behind. Dylan was like a little spy and would tell Mum and Dad everything. If he wasn't he was copying me and getting me caught for something I shouldn't of been doing such as playing by the stream at the golf course on the way to and from school. It didn't matter what we were doing, whether what we were doing was right or wrong, we almost always argued. No matter what it was, it was my fault in the eyes of my parents. I always felt he was favoured over me. I was the eldest and held accountable for all the mistakes regardless if they were mines or not. Dylan had a temper, a short fuse and was very confrontational. He got violent with me on numerous occasions when things didn't go his way between us.

On one occasion we had come home from school for lunch and Dad had nipped out to pick Mum up for work. Being left in the house for short periods of time wasn't something uncommon back then. I can't remember what the argument was about but I ended up barricading myself in his bedroom using a set of step ladders that had been sitting outside the bedroom door for access to the attic, placing them against the door to stop him getting in. He had chased me through the house and up the stairs with a golf club wanting to smash my head in with it. When he got in to the room he took a swing at me missing and smashing the light bulb hanging from the ceiling. It was my fault of course. I was the eldest and should have known better. He was only about 5 or 6 years old at the time and I was a little terrified of him when he lost his temper. Years later a friend saved me from his temper when something hadn't gone his way, he straddled me inside a pitched tent in a friends back garden. He wrapped his hands around my throat to choke me. I felt the air disappear from within me as I struggled to push his body weight off from on top of me. It was the closest I had ever felt to death then and even now to this day. One of our friends had come into the tent we were in and seeing what he was doing to me they dragged him off of my almost lifeless body shouting at him that it was only a game but unable to reason with him. I was gasping for air, too scared to tell my parents as I would probably be the one who got into trouble.

We did occasionally have our good times as we were growing up. We would have sleepovers in each of our bedrooms. We would make dens with covers and sleep in them. We saved our pocket money to buy jars of Nutella chocolate spread, eating it with a spoon while we had picnics in our den. For supper we would have piles of toast cut into either triangles of squares. Dylan would call it half cooked toast as it was barely toasted, just the way he liked it. I have very few happy memories of us when we were younger, not arguing. But despite all our faults and the arguments as we grew up, I know he would do anything for me and my family now. It's like an unspoken bond, a respect in one another that's never said.

Gregor and Sophie lived nearby. They were our cousins, their Dad being my dad's twin brother. Gregor was a year older than me and Sophie a year younger. Our dads would take us swimming in Perth and I loved it. Sophie was taking figure skating classes and we would go and watch her class then take to the rink for a skate ourselves. I wasn't really any good at it but the rush when Dad took one hand and my Uncle the other was exhilarating, pulling me around the rink at full pelt. When Dylan and I stayed over I had fun, the sort of fun that I suppose any child would have when they have a sleepover, just like the fun my own kids have today, a different bed, different rules and with friends or in my case my cousins. Their house always had a smell of curry and booze. Uncle Sam liked a drink and would always be either cooking Indian curries or ordering in Indian takeaways. I would sleep with Sophie downstairs and Dylan with Gregor upstairs. The only thing that I really didn't like was that they all slept in the dark, not even a hall way light was left on for going to the toilet. I hated the dark. We had been allowed to watch the film 'Gremlins' one night and I was petrified at bed time. Gregor sneaked down stairs and made horrible noises pretending to be a gremlin making me cry most of that night as I watched the shadows that formed on the bedroom walls from the street lights outside.

Sophie and I got to go to the Rollarama at the community centre just around the corner from their house on a Friday night. All my friends would be there, skating around in circles listening to all our favourite songs. 'London nights' by the London Boys, was a huge hit at the time. The lights would be dimmed only the disco lights and the light from the tuck shop area to see where you were going. A Dj was tucked in the corner of the hall and stairs led to the seating area where we would socialise with our friends.

I don't really remember a time when Mum was the one looking after us as children. Mum was the bread winner in the house. She had a full time position at our local Asda store. Dad had at some point after we moved back to Dundee had an accident at work. He had been a fully trained baker and his accident had meant that he could no longer work. I'm sure he must have been really frustrated having to live the way we did as I could often tell in his temper. I was always terrified when we had done something wrong and Mum said to us "wait till you Dad gets home". I don't blame him in any way for being the way he was with us as the good times always outweighed the bad and it taught us a sense of respect. We in no way got away with murder and I just had to see the change of mood in his eyes to want to vacate the room.

Despite the arguments with my brother and the constant feeling of him being favoured, life was great in the early days but an unexpected dark cloud was looming over us, a catalyst in shaping the rest of my life. Everything as I had known it was to come to a sudden end. It was all changing and I was completely helpless. I was scared, lost and alone and I felt completely invisible as it unfolded in front of my eyes.

" Someone once gave me a box full of darkness. It took me years to understand that this too, was a gift" _Mary Oliver

Chapter Three

We lived in what seemed like a quiet little cul-de-sac in Kirkton, Dundee. The community mostly knew each other and most of the children in the area were friends of mine. A family which had been friends of Mum and Dad's had family throughout the neighbourhood that were involved in things that were certainly not in any way lawful. One night my parents became witness to something that I'm sure to this day they wished they hadn't.

These family members were seen in the middle of the street making petrol bombs in the boot of a car, with the intent to bomb the family around the corner who owned the local corner shop. Mum and Dad couldn't just sit back and ignore what they were seeing, so they made what was meant to be an anonymous phone call to the police. When local officers turned up at our front door for all to see it was obvious who had tipped them off. It was a decision that saved the family who they had intended to torture that night but it was to ultimately alter the course of all our lives. It was the beginning of a nightmare that would last for months even years long after that one phone call.

Witnesses to a crime, Mum and Dad were to appear in court. The days and months leading up to the court date, life was made almost impossible for our whole family. People were scared to associate with us and most of my friends disserted me. For our own safety school hours were altered. We entered 15 minutes behind everyone and left for home 15minutes in front. School had become like a prison where my friends were no longer friends but fellow prisoners out to make my life hell. Mum got harassed at her work resulting in the whole family who were torturing us to be banned from their local Asda store. People became nasty meaning it was no longer safe to play freely in our neighbourhood.

Dad would attend local neighbourhood watch meetings but even there people couldn't speak their mind freely because of the gossips who would pass on information that had been entrusted to the group.

One night while lying in bed, Dad at his usual meeting just around the corner from our house, a riot broke out in our street. Suddenly there were police everywhere, in the street, in our house and even in the sky. My brother and I were sent to my parent's room upstairs. We lay there in my parent's bed the safest room in the house because the bed was nowhere near the window. We didn't know what could end up going through it as a brick flying through the windows wasn't something uncommon. Getting out wasn't an option, the street was cornered off with no way in or out. A house full of CID wasn't uncommon either but on this particular night things got really scary. I recall the sound of the rioting outside and the helicopter flying by waving the bright light that beamed in the bedroom window as it passed, police speaking through voice amplifiers and my Mum's cries. I was so scared that night, having only the comfort of seeing the police officers walk back and forth past the bedroom doorway as they checked up on us and used the bathroom next door.

The days, week's even months that followed were not any better. Dad's car which was usually parked in our driveway was on numerous occasions vandalised. Slashed tires, smashed windows and even paint stripper over the bonnet. Things were smashed through the living room window, Dads garden trashed, his vegetable patch ripped to shreds, the shed set on fire. And mostly all happened while we all slept in our beds at night. Seeing Dad's anger every time his pride and joys was diminished was hurtful and made me even a little scared of him. He didn't keep well at the best of times, not with the accident he had at work when I was young.

On many occasions my brother and I were sent away to stay with family, often my Gran who meant the world to me. It was safer that way. We eventually joined another school closer to my Grans so that we could go there while we stayed and feel safe but I hated it. I hated it so much as I didn't properly understand why our lives were turning upside down. I didn't want my life to be changing so rapidly. I now know it was the only way to get an education and be safe. The new school was cold and old fashioned and I couldn't understand why the boys played in a separate playground from the girls. I was so nervous that first day, I didn't know anybody there apart from my brother who was two years below me. Cleppington Primary school was an old school. My Dad had attended it when he was a young boy. The old stone steps that twisted as I climbed them each day to reach my classroom at the top of the building were old and worn. Everything looking back just seemed so grey, so dull and so cold, a reflection of my state of mind at the time. In the end we didn't stay very long. Well not long enough to make any friends.

One night before my brother and I had moved into my Grans on a more permanent basis, I recall a noise at my bedroom window. It wasn't unusual for one of our cats to be making a noise needing me to open the window to let them in so not thinking I opened the curtains not excepting to see a man waving and screaming at me. I was terrified as the screaming broke out when my parents realised someone was in the garden being threatening. It was an image that has haunted me all these years.

It got so bad that Dad and Uncle Sam would have to take shifts staying up all night in the dark with baseball bats, metal bars and the likes. Just waiting for them to come, doing whatever necessary to protect us and our property. Nothing seemed to stop them. There was a house with occupants between ours and the first house that the family occupied but even that didn't stop them trying to gain access to our house through the attics, nothing could keep us safe. We had the extra security of our Dobermans, Sheeba and Max but even that didn't stop them, their kennel outside burnt to the ground.

When it eventually came to the court case Mum and Dad had to get police escorts to and from the court. They had to sit at opposite ends of the cafeteria with officers, entered the court room via the cells so not to pass the family in the corridors. It must have been a nightmare for them. The accused were found guilty but while in the custody of the police officers through in Arbroath, the accused jumped over the wall at the police station while being escorted. He had his uncle waiting in the wings to pick him up and bring him back to Dundee where he could hide him. He had drained the water from his water tank making what he thought a perfect hiding place. He escaped to the roof tops once found and the street was yet again cornered off. Police dogs, police cars and cid with voice amplifiers were all something I remember from that day. There were loads of people out in the street witnessing the whole thing and I watched him as he hid behind the chimney amongst all the carnage on the street below.

Breaking point came in the shade of paint stripper, pored all over the bonnet of Dad's car sitting in the drive while we slept. He could take no more. We were taken from our sleep in the early hours, packed into a car with smashed glass rattling about on the parcel shelf behind us. We were taken straight to our Grans, our sanctuary. Never again were we to call Dundee home. It hadn't felt like home for so long.

Dad had taken all the grief that was humanly possible for one man to take and had flipped. He had to disappear, needed space to calm down before he did something he would regret. Uncle Sam and Mum single-handedly emptied our house of our belongings all the while fighting against the abuse and vile mouths as they tried to pack up the removal van. Belongings were stolen from the removal van as they tried to pack them and in the end so much was left behind. They just couldn't pack it all in the time scale, couldn't be harassed no longer, we needed to get out of our nightmare.

The council were of no use, wouldn't help Mum and Dad get a new house. In the end it took for them to come to breaking point to just up and leave, do a moonlight flit with no new home to go to. We were homeless. My Aunty kindly took us in while my Uncle was away with the Marines. They had three children who I didn't really know that well. My cousins were a lot younger than me but it was company, a child form of company I hadn't had for a long time. What stuff Mum and Uncle Sam had managed to pack was put into storage and we managed to live with just the bare essentials.

I was so lost at that point, felt like a shell of a person. I had lost my home, my friends, pets that I adored had to be given away because we no longer had a home and I was farer away from my Gran who had been a huge part of my brother and I's everyday life. I didn't like it at all. I didn't know Arbroath, lots of new streets, new faces. The only up side was that there was lots of exploring to do but I wasn't to let anyone know who I was. I had been warned not to tell anyone who I was, not to tell them what had happened to us. Everyone was scared that they would find us. I wasn't allowed to think about it let alone tell anyone. Starting all over again, making a new identity for myself, made to forget my past. Something that I could pretend to do but secretly I would cry at night, grieving for the life that was. I know now that it was for my own safety.

Most of my belongings remained in storage until we eventually got re homed. The police had to step in to get us re-housed, a house that was to be seen as a safe house. Luckily it was nearby to my Aunties. I started back at school half way through P6 and I hated it to start with. New faces, feeling like the odd one out as everyone had already bonded and made friendships over the last 6 years. Friendships like the ones I once had but wasn't to speak off. Slowly I began to make friends but they weren't close friends. I would always feel like the spare part in the group, the third wheel that didn't quite work or fit in.

I would day dream about my past, dreamed of going back to see my friends, to see what had become of my home. It was a dream that I never got the opportunity to do until I was a teenager. It was a trip with a friend that didn't really understand the history, the feelings that at that point had been buried for years. It was a secret that nobody truly understood but me.

At nights for years afterwards and even to this very day I dream about going back. The contents of the dream always vary in form but a constant always remains. I am back at my old neighbourhood and I'm looking straight at my house. Sometimes it looks different inside and out but

I know where I am. I walk up to the door and it opens welcoming me inside. Other times I watch it from afar and try to get a sense as to why it looks so different and why other people are inside. There are dreams when I move back into my old home with my parents but I have a sense of worry as I have left my own children and husband back in our existing home and don't know how to get back to them. Then there are the nightmares where I am trapped in my old home with ghosts who want to hurt me. I feel trapped, bars on the window and feet stuck to the floor as I scream for my children and husband. My unconscious mind likes to relive this small part of me on a regular basis and I still don't know why.

I had become very withdrawn and shy after all that had happened. I had lost all the confidence that oozed out of me just years previously. Boyfriends could off come so easy being the new face in a school. I can recall a few that showed interest. Although it was appealing I felt like I had died inside. I wasn't allowed to be my true self. I had to hide a side of me that had shaped who I was, a past that no longer existed.

I would put on a façade, tried to forget and get on with my life. I would play in the cemetery behind my house with new friends. Funny considering how I was feeling inside. We would climb trees in the cemetery and play our kiss and tell games. "You've to kiss for sixty seconds and use tongues" they would say as we played our games. It was fun and exciting in a way I hadn't felt in such a long time but I was so confused about my life and who I was supposed to be. It was during these moments while playing that I was beginning to feel again what it was like to be a child. The kiss and tell games we played while we were young are a far cry away from the woman I am today. They were a process that took my mind off my old life. They made me quizzical about what came next, the start of a process that leaded to my desperation to be noticed, to be liked and to be loved.

"This is my carefree, this is my freedom – this is MY HAPPY" _Coco J. Ginger

Chapter Four

My Gran was an amazing woman. In my eyes she was Wonder Woman. I spent a lot of time as a young girl resting, playing and just enjoying my grandparents company, my Grans especially. I learned a lot from my Gran. She was a very social person often taking me out to see different friends and attending social events. I loved how she presented herself. She had a powerful owe about her, a very loving character. When we weren't out socialising we would be busy in the house or in the garden on a nice day, sitting in the sun, a floral covered cushion between my backside and the cold tiled doorstep. Sipping on Coke floats and eating Lemonade ice lollies, the smell of sweets as they were being made from Keilors, the sweet factory at their back door. I loved moments like that, so blissful, not a care in the world.

We would hop on a bus right outside the house and be taken down town, right to The Form Centre. Lunch was a great treat, usually in the department store, Arnotts, going up in the lifts, passing all the smells from the perfume stalls to the little coffee shop near the top of the building. If we weren't in there for lunch it was in BHS café in the Wellgate where Gran's brother worked or in C&A's. We would have a look around all the outlet shops in The Form centre, one of them being some sort of food store where they sold dried foods. I loved the Bombay mix. Before we caught the bus back home we would go into The Early Learning Centre where I would always be treated with new arts and craft stuff to keep me occupied when we got home.

We would go for a walks to Stopswell. To the post office where I always got some new writing pencil or writing pad, had a noisy in the cheap shop across the road. Then we would come home with yummy freshly made bridies from the bakers for everyone's lunch.

Coffee mornings were really common too. There was a white building to the right of The Wellgate centre down town, still stands there today. We would bake loads of yummy goodies and take them down to sell. Gran would sit and have coffee with friends and I got to wonder around looking at the jumble sale stuff, buying little made up bags of penny sweets.

I had been fairly young when I visited the dental hospital, my back teeth having to be removed. Sitting in the waiting room, feeling very nervous, not knowing exactly what they were going to do to me was probably my first memory of uncertainness. I had to lie down on a bed while they placed a black mask over my face, counting from 10 back to 1 but only getting to 9. Afterwards I spent the night at my Grans. As I lay in her double bed next to her I recall the warmness of the company and the hot water bottles. Gran and Grandad went to bed each night with several hot water bottles and I grew to love the comfort of their heat. The room would be peaceful all but the sound of Gran reading her daily newspapers, a small light shun behind us from the built in headboard, two small pull cords to switch them on and off. I would get to do the puzzles, spot the difference and spot the ball. Once the lights went out I would listen to the cars pass by in the street outside and from the busy Kingsway only a street away. Car head lights would shine through the top of the curtains, my eyes following them as they danced across the ceiling. I loved nights when I got to sleep in the same bed as my Gran, she would have her side and I would mine. Grandad had as long as I can remember, slept in a single bed in the other bedroom. As I got older I would get to sleep in his bed when he was in hospital or respite care. Eventually the giant table in the dining room was replaced with a sofa bed which was where I would sleep over when I had friends staying over with me. Gran always opened her house to guests and I loved her for that.

As I got a little older, Gran would trust me to nip to the local shop for the odd bit of groceries if she needed them, usually getting to keep the change to spend on sweets. We would take Kimmy, Grans sheep dog and tie her up outside.

Granddad god bless his soul, had a heart of gold but was a grump at the best of times, wasn't scared to speak his mind and always had something to complain about, whether it was the racket the neighbours were making, something on the television he didn't like or Black People as he would call them, didn't much like foreigners. He was most likely found either in the kitchen doing dishes, in his shed pottering about with his tools fixing something or in his chair watching television, reading his paper or sleeping upright. He loved his football, wrestling and snooker and l loved to sit and watch the snooker with him as I found it really relaxing. He was funny at times to say the least. When the cats were in the garden he would sit and throw stones at them from his bedroom window and fill Dylan's Super Soaker water pistol to soak the "wee buggers" as he would call them. He had been an electrical engineer by trade, working in a garage all his life, often found outside pottering about with Dad at the car. He loved taking Kimmy for her walks, the image of him with his walking stick, blue jacket, his tammy on and torch in hand is an image I'll never forget. He always had a torch at hand, a character and a half.

Benny lived down stairs from Gran. I suppose you could say that he was my first boyfriend. Not in a girlfriend/boyfriend term but someone I hung out with. He was the first friend that I made while spending time at my grandparents. When it was nice we would be out in the paddling pool, running about and sunbathing on the sun loungers, sometimes playing indoors at his house. I remember his walls being painted dark blue all over and rockets and stars were painted on the walls and ceiling. Playing with a wide up toy in the shape of a television, I'm sure its tune was 'London's Bridge is falling down'. I missed him when he moved away.

Our cousins Gregor and Sophie would sometimes stay when Dylan and I stayed, our parents most likely out having a good time. I don't ever remember thinking about what they were up to, I was just happy to be in the company of my Gran. When we were all there we would sleep in the living room, taking the sofa cushions off and using them to make dens and sleep in them. The coo-coo clock that chimed on the hr every hr was a comforting sound. I was fascinated by it and the sound it made in the quiet.

I always felt like my Grans favourite but she probably wouldn't have admitted it in front of anyone so not to upset them. She made me feel loved, feel useful and needed. She taught me how to bake, we would make wonderful things. People always came to visit and we made afternoon tea from scratch, all nicely positioned on platters and stands. I'll never forget the smell as she made frying steak for dinner and the home cooked meals that she made for everyone, all sat round the large dining table. The family always went to Grans sometimes even for breakfast, dinner and tea. The house was always so full of life, always people visiting, a place of peace and comfort, the heart of the family.

We would spend endless hours doing all sorts of arts and crafts. Knitting, sewing, drawing, writing, make and do. We even made our own play dough which I loved the smell off. I could make it any colour I wished. She taught me how to clean, to iron and even paint. I learned so many skills as a child that I am so grateful to her for now as an adult.

I remember my grandparents dancing around the living room, twirling and laughing to the sound of "Donald where's your trousers" They were so happy and in love. They would pull me up to join them. I loved how they would always keep me involved with what they were doing. I never felt left out.

We would go out for walks, taking Kimmy the sheepdog with us, running through piles of autumn leaves kicking them up into the air, splashing in the puddles, skipping along, the fresh air and feeling of freedom. I would collect snails found crawling up lampposts when it was damp outside, put them in a plastic pot or jar with holes in them to breath, filled with lettuce and grass. Gross now looking back but I saw them as my little pets. We would take Kimmy to Caird Park, take fishing nets with us and dip for tadpoles in the pond, gather up fallen acorns and golf balls that had wondered from the golf course. Betty and Harry were really good friends of Grans. They stayed on the Kingsway, not far from Gran and Granddad's house. On Saturday nights we would take Kimmy out for a walk and end up at their house. Gran and Grandad would have a drink and I would get lemonade and biscuits. We would play pitch and putt in their back garden, sit and play games. I can still remember them to this day, long after they passed away, Betty busy in the kitchen with her apron on, Harry in his chair by the window reading his paper, the smell of old people in their house, but a comforting smell.

After a long day of activities we would settle down, Granddad on his seat, Gran and myself on the couch. We would watch TV, 'Beauty and the beast', 'Baywatch 'and 'Catchphrase' were my favourites. Gran would make us all supper then we would relax. She would gently stroke my arm till I was almost sleeping. I loved the feeling of it. I felt relaxed, safe and so happy. I always felt secure while staying over. I would lie in bed, in the spare room and snuggle down. Sometimes I would sneak out of bed and lie down in front of the gas fire with a blanket. The warmth was like no other I've felt before or since. I was oblivious of everything around me, just so happy and no longer worrying about the hassle that I had left back home. I didn't have to face that, not now, not until I was back, back in a whirl wind of anger, of what felt like prison.

When we did the moon light flit I didn't see my Gran near as much as I had before. I eventually started to grow up and our time together wasn't the same as it had been when I was younger. I would visit almost every week when I wasn't at school and I always knew that she loved me. If I could go back and spend all that time with her all over again I would in a flash.

"One night when we were lying under the stars together she pointed to this beaming bright star beside the moon and said wherever she was in the world, whether we were together or apart, that I should remember her with that star because it would always be there–that it was her with me".

_Rebecah McManus

"Do not let another day go by where your dedication to other people's opinions is greater than your dedication to your own emotions!"
_Steve Maraboli

Chapter Five

I loved the school holidays when I was younger, long before the dark cloud had been cast over our heads. We would be out on our bikes, exploring, making dens and playing in each other's houses. We went to holiday clubs at the 'Dick Mctaggart Centre' in Kirkton. A friend, Nikki and I would make up dance routines to Madonna's 'True blue' a song we both loved. I had heard stories about the fictional character Freddy Krueger from the movies 'Nightmare on Elm Street'. Having an overactive imagination we would make up stories about him being in the shower room where the toilets were at the centre. Believing our own tales we would have to run through the shower rooms to get the toilet at the other side or risk holding it in until we got home.

We would spend our pocket money at the shops and explore past the boundaries that we had been set by our parents. "Don't go to that burn" they would say. Of course we would never listen. What they didn't know didn't hurt unless of course we fell in and had to go home soaking wet and explain ourselves. A thick ear and grounding was to be had.

My cousins from up north would come down to stay during holidays and I loved it when the adults had a night of drinking. We would usually get to stay out later and we were almost every time guaranteed the left over Chinese. I loved it even more when we went to visit them up north. I hated the car journey; I always got travel sickness and still to this day hate travelling. My brother and I would be sprawled across the back seats playing magnetic travel games. There weren't car seats in them days or seat belts in the back seats. I loved the music my parents played. To this day, every time I hear Elton John's 'Island girl' or 'Lucy in the sky with diamonds', I'm brought back in time.

The view is spectacular but I never really noticed it until I was older.

I always feel like I going home when we visit. A lot has changed but the smell always remains the same. You just can't beat the smell of a coal burning fire on a cold day and the purity smell of nature that the Scottish Highlands oozes. That's one of the things that make Kinlochleven so special for me as well as my family ties to its special place.

I was always closer to my cousin Danielle rather than her younger sister Holly. I suppose it was because we were the same age only she was one month older. We would play in the woods and get to go to the shops for sweets. There was a river on the other side of the woods. We weren't allowed to go there but who ever listened to their parents, really? We did get caught a few times usually when one of our younger brothers had followed us and fell in trying to copy us on the stepping stones. You don't seem to have a sense of fear in that way when younger. I guess that's why we always did things we weren't meant to and why my brother always seemed to be needing stitches after doing something stupid. They were spoil sports but I know now as a parent myself that they were only trying to protect us.

The sound of water rushing by cleansing everything in its path, the birds you cannot see chirping in the trees above, the warmth on your skin from the sun beaming down on you from the heavens above, reflecting off the stream like millions of tiny diamonds, all pure and blissful. These were moments in time when everything ceased to exist. Times when I was alone, times when everyone was busy so I would go for a walk and find that special place where I could switch off completely.

I was a dreamer as a child, always thinking and dreaming about life. I still am when I get the time. Moments where life seems to stand still are all too rare when you're an adult. Always something needing done, some chore, some problem to be fixed. I would zone out, feel at peace, relaxed like I was on another planet. Those were the times when I had no worries, no problems in my head.

I've always had a good imagination, from strutting my stuff in front of the mirror with a hairbrush, dreaming that I was an amazing pop star, everyone in owe of me, to playing different scenarios with my Barbie dolls. I was creative and understood that from an early age, always being told so in report cards from school. I loved the film 'Dirty dancing' and would spend hours imagining that I was Baby. I wanted to be her, to dance like her and to be touched by someone just like Patrick Swayze does her. I would move my hips and pretend I was carrying the watermelon ready to join in with all the sweating and grinding that went on behind closed doors. It was so sexy. I wanted the love and all that came with it. In the school playground I would dramatically start signing 'Totally devoted to you' from the movie Grease, one of my top ten favourite movies from my childhood.

Organising pretend marriages between myself and my at the time boyfriend and friends was a school playtime game. There was two very tall trees at the corner of our playground were we would hold the ceremonies. I would wear my white lace gloves and have a wee handbag and a toy ring, a new boy accessory each week. Boyfriends back then were like toys, a past time. They would last a day or two and then you would move on, swap about a bit with friends then take them back again. Then one of them moved school and I felt lost for the first time. Kristian was his name. I had a horrible feeling in the pit of my stomach, held onto a goodbye picture he gave me before he left. I cried into my pillow listening to 'she's like the wind' from Dirty dancing. It was an emotion I hadn't encountered before. It opened the flood gates with the first glimpse of my hormones. I was only 8/9yrs old.

I heard on the news that Freddy Mercury had died, I had no idea how or why it had happened but I felt so emotional. I didn't even know him, another sign that something in me was changing.

Then I got shipped up to Grans house. Something wasn't right with Mum. All I knew was that they were going up north. It was just before Christmas and all the houses were decorated with fairy lights. It was cold outside, snow on the hills. I started listening in on phone calls to get an idea of what's going on. Grandpa had died.

Knew he wasn't well but didn't know it was so serious. I had visited him in hospital in Inverness while he was getting treatment. He was wearing his blue tammy and a massive smile, my last memory of him. I would cry at night for him when no one was watching or listening, hiding my emotions from others. Something I continued to do right till adulthood and even to this day. I didn't want to be seen as weak.

"The best thing about a picture is that it never changes, even when the people in it do" _Andy Warhol

Chapter Six

Starting secondary school was like having to start all over again, new faces, new surroundings a yet another new routine. You would think I had grown accustom to this with everything that had happened up to now but It was hard. Trying to make new friends again, I had no confidence, no self-a-steam. At 11/12 yrs old I was a lost child looking for a sense of belonging.

The first few weeks were full of apprehension, walking into new classrooms not knowing if there was going to be anyone there I knew. Who was I going to sit beside? Who was I going to speak to at break time? In registration class I met this girl. She was so full of life and seemed to know who she was and what she wanted. She was friendly and it was so nice to have someone to speak to. She became one of my closest friends, my best friend. We did everything together. Our dads were fishing mates and through their friendships we grew even closer. We were carefree and young and I began to love life again. She introduced something back to me I had lost for a while. We went through all lives ups and downs together as we could rely on one another. For a long time we were inseparable.

During weekends and holidays we would go through to my Grans for a break. I loved the freedom we had, going down town to spend our money on pop socks and short dresses, visiting the cinema to see the film 'Maverick', eyeing up the guys at Camperdown park then walking home stopping by the old Chinese takeaway that Mum and Dad had used when we had stayed in Dundee.

Gran had taught me how to make cakes using colours, cutting and layering them so that when you sliced into them they were chequered. I used this technique to make a special cake on one of our visits for Megan's birthday.

Megan and I both went through a stage of loving Meatloaf, were constantly listening to 'Bat out of hell'. I'm sure her favourite was 'Two out of three aint bad'. We had so much in common, I felt secure with her. I was able to speak to her about all sorts of stuff so it was only natural that she became the first to learn about my past. I had never told anyone to this day the full extent of our ordeal but she was there for me when I wanted to go back, when I finally felt save enough to let someone see a small piece of who I was. I wanted to see my old neighbourhood. I needed some form of closure after being whisked away so quickly.

"A true friend is someone who sees the pain in your eyes while everyone else believes your smile"

It was a lovely sunny day as we walked down towards my old neighbourhood, stopping by the stream that I used to play at when I was younger, even though I got told not to. The street was just as I remembered it, young children playing in it like I used to do. We walked right up to the front gate of my old house and all the while my heart was thumping. Would any of my old neighbours and friends still reside in the street? Would anyone know who I was and would I see any of my old friends? My old home had new tenants that had looked after the house. New windows and doors had been fitted and a caravan was now parked on the driveway that Dad had built. We walked for hours throughout all the streets that I used to play, past Gillburn primary school, where I had such a happy childhood in the beginning, to the shops where I would spend my tuck money for school, to all the parks I would play and to Asda where Mum had once worked. So many memories all swirling around in my head, scared at the thought of bumping into someone I knew but at the same time hopeful that I would. I always wondered if people remembered who I was. Was I just a name with a face that faded over time? How was I remembered? The names of my old friends were still clearly embedded in my mind but their faces had faded over the years. Maybe if I had bumped into anyone I wouldn't off known them anyway.

I had shared a small part of my secret with my best friend who was there for me not fully understanding what was really going on in my head. I was grateful for finally having someone to speak to.

It was another beautiful day outside, the day I returned the favour. I still remember the fear and pain as I held her tight the day she thought her dad had died. Our dads had gone away on a fishing trip together but for some reason my Dad didn't get on the boat, had come home. When the boat had gone missing and all aboard couldn't be found, she ran all the way from her house to mine in her bare feet to await the fate of all on board. Soon the wreck was found but the men aboard were found one by one, their life stolen away from them. We got news of this and soon Megan found out that the man she knew as her uncle was one of them. We feared for her dad as he was the last to be discovered. Eventually and with a lot of luck and praying he was found, the sole survivor of the tragedy. The funeral for her Uncle that followed was the first I'd ever been too and I held her hand tight. Let her know I was right there with her.

Megan and I shared everything, from getting the same school clothes as each other at the start of the new term to listening to the same music. Elton John's' I guess that why they call it the blues' was another favourite. We had very similar tastes in boys which at first was ok. It was just silly infatuations with boys we had met on holiday at first, ones that didn't show any interest back other than friendship. All was ok until one much closer to home actually became keen on one of us. Danny was his name and Megan had grown fascinated with him. Megan and I had started to drift apart by this point, she had started to hang around with other people at school and I had once again become a bit of a loner. I would wander the corridors at school during break times with no body to speak to, often found sat in the corridor of the second floor instead of the common area or school gates where everyone else who was cool was to be found. I was once again a lost soul desperate for some attention from someone, just anyone who was keen enough to speak back. When Danny wanted to go out with me I jumped at the opportunity, I liked him and he liked me. If Megan and I had been closer I would never of considered it but she had no time for me anymore, I was a loner and someone wanted to be with me, even if it was some silly little boy/girl crush that went nowhere fast. It in hindsight was the decision that pushed Megan and I further apart even though our relationship was already heading in that direction.

I find it strange how friendships drift in and out of our lives, most only in it for a small part but always long enough to make an ever lasting impression. Some people are lucky to have the friendships that last for a life time but I was never lucky enough to find such ones. People drifted in and out of my life all the time. People moved on and made new friends. We always grew apart and went in different directions in life.

Dawn was my next door neighbour. We became friends shortly after we had moved and settled into Arbroath. She was a year older than me and at a different school across town. We would hang out together after school and sometimes at weekends. We went from playing with Barbie dolls together to stealing alcohol from my Gran's house and getting blind drunk at the age of 13. In the early days we would make up dance routines for going around houses guising, played hunt with all the other neighbourhood kids, played Kirby at the roadside and took part in summertime water fights in the street with our other neighbour Lily who lived across the road from us both. As we got a little older the Barbie dolls and Trolls that we collected and played with became a thing of the past. We started hanging out at the park across the back from us, mucked about doing all the silly crazes like putting Vicks vapour rub on our eyes to make ourselves cry to sniffing marker pens.

I was invited to stay at one of her friends houses one night. I remember being a little nervous about going as I didn't know her friends from school. In the end it wasn't your typical sleepover, It turned out to be a party with boys staying over which made me feel even more uncomfortable. I didn't know this when it had first been arranged and didn't like lying to my parents about who I was with. I wanted to go home that night but Dawn told me to stop being silly, that my parents wouldn't find out about who was there. I spent the night feeling slightly intimidated as the guys were older and I didn't know anyone bar Dawn who was too fascinated with the one guy she fancied to see that I just wanted to go home. The girls had put dog food into the sandwiches that they fed to the guys so they were out for revenge that night. I was too scared to sleep, scared of what they would do. Some guy ended up with marker pen all over his face and body, unable to scrub it all off in the shower the next morning.

Soon I was learning the act of lying and stretching the truth. Dawn had introduced me to alcohol, had managed to get it for us from her older friends. She had encouraged me to steal some while staying at my Grans house one weekend, pouring a bit of this and a bit of that into empty juice bottles, making lethal concoctions. We stashed it in our bags and went down to the Vicky Park that night. We had two bottles of mixed up pure spirit and drank the lot. I was feeling slightly tipsy but Dawn began to fall all over the place, falling into hedges as we walked home drunk, getting caught by her mum and step dad when we arrived back to hers for the night. I was grounded for a month after our little experiment. I didn't learn though.

Violet was an old friend from primary school who would sometimes hang out with us. We would often hang out at Violet's drinking vodka and fresh orange juice out of Wimpy cups from where Violets family worked before heading out to the under 18's Ballies. We would stay over at Violets and go down to the Wimpy in the morning for freshly made donuts. The Wimpy also became the place to go on a school day for lunch as we would either get it for free or at a reduced price.

There was this one night that we decided to camp out at what's called Death Valley. It wasn't far from home but far enough for us to think we were cool. Jake a friend from school snuck up on us throwing stones at our tent frightening the life out of us. So much so that Violet ended completely out of her sleeping bag and into mine. It rained like hell that night and somehow I got left that morning to carry all our stuff home. I'm sure I fell out with them over it.

"Happiness is not to be found at the bottom of a bottle or from the tip of a needle; it is not to be found admist a cloud of smoke or within a sugar coated pill. If you look for it in these places, you will find naught but despair." _Gerald Trotman

My cousin Gregor had been in a lot of trouble at home, his mum didn't want him staying at hers and nor did his dad. He came to live with us for a while, had been given his final chance. He enrolled in the same school as us and Mum and Dad even adapted the house by converting the attic so that he had his own room. At first I thought it was cool to have him staying but it turned into a nightmare when he got involved with the wrong crowd and ended up on drugs. From that started the downward spiral of stealing, lying and basically being a horrible person. It caused a lot of strain on my parents and the house became a tense place to live again. It caused many an argument between my parents and I remember coming home from school one day to a load of commotion. Dad was angry, Mum was crying and our neighbours who were close friends had been the ones who sorted it all out. The fridge door had a massive dent in it so I can only imagine the argument that I had missed. Mum was at breaking point and he had to go. When he did our home was a much happier place to be. I only saw him a few times years after he left. He was unrecognisable, face all drawn in, teeth all missing or what was left were black, fag hanging out his mouth and clothes hanging off him. He had asked my old friend Megan for my address. I felt bad not allowing him to have it but I had seen him pass my house so many times, I could see clearly that he was still on drugs. I didn't want to be the next family member to fall victim to his crimes. It was sad to see what had become of my cousin who I had once been so close with. His sister Sophie, I lost contact with when she went to stay with her mum when their parent's marriage fell apart. It was years later that we found each other on Facebook. She seems to be doing really well for herself but we have never seen each other in person since before we moved to Arbroath.

"I wonder if this is how people get close: They heal each other's wounds; they repair the broken skin" _Lauren Oliver

At the age of 14 I met a guy who I was in owe of. He was a year younger than me but he fascinated me. Max had a passion for music and loved playing on his decks. He introduced me to dance music and we would sit for hours chilled out in his room with his strobe light on. He was the first guy to passionately kiss me with his tongue and I just couldn't get enough of kissing him. It made me tingle deep inside, I felt alive. We would kiss for hours on top of his bunk bed and on the living room floor watching movies while his mum was out. I felt comfortable with him when we were alone, comfortable enough to allow him to put his hands in my pants, to penetrate me with his fingers.

When we weren't alone there was usually a group of girls hanging about one of which fancied him but it felt great to be able to say that he was mine. I don't remember how it ended but I remember him moving shortly afterwards. He had distracted me from all the tension my cousin was causing back home before he was chucked out and I was distracting him from his parent's recent break up.

I saw him one night in a nightclub shortly after I got married. He introduced me to his friend as his first girlfriend. It was lovely to see him but I would put money on it that he is now gay. At least I got that impression from him that night when we bumped into each other. It would of been nice to exchange numbers to see what became of him but having just got married I didn't want to rock the boat and give him the wrong impression.

" It was the first time she'd discovered something she really didn't want to find, and she didn't know what to do once she'd found it" _Jodi Picoult

Chapter Seven

Our street was full of children of all different ages but we never let our ages get in the way of us all being friendly. When Dawn or Lily weren't available to come out and play there was always someone else around to hang out with and play Kirby with. The family across the road from us had four children, a son my age, two younger, a boy and a girl and one slightly older son. Kyle, the eldest son when around with his friends would join in on our friendly games of Hunt. Hunt was a combination of the games hide and seek and chase. One person counted while everyone else ran and hid in the street. Once found you had to run away and try and get back to the den before the person caught you.

While playing Hunt one night some guy a little older decided to corner me. I had never met him before but he was Kyle's friend. He chased me passed the boundaries of our game and around the corner until I was out of breath. I felt threatened. I didn't know nor trust this guy. My instincts were right not to. I still remember his grubby touch as he pinned me to the hedge and put his hand up my skirt. Tears were flooding into my mouth drowning my screams as he tried to get into my pants. Almost like a guardian angel Kyle pulled him off me, kicked him to the kerb screaming at him, saying what? I can't remember for the shaking and tears deafening me. I went home that night and didn't say a word, crawled into bed feeling dirty, it was never mentioned again.

Through Kyle I got to know Sam and his friend Gavin. Sam's mum and step dad had moved into our street. His step dad was an old fishing friend of my Dad's and soon our Mums got friendly. Sam and I somehow ended up a couple to my parents dislike. I don't know why they didn't like him but I felt like they were always trying to keep us apart. I was always getting grounded so he would come to my window at night with love notes and serenade me with Bon Jovi songs.

"Sex isn't good unless it means something. It doesn't necessarily need to mean 'love' and it doesn't necessarily need to happen in a relationship, but it does need to mean intimacy and connect..... There exists a very fine line between being sexually liberated and being sexually used" _Laura Sessions Stepp

It was the 1st of January just before my 15th birthday and Sam and I were left alone at his house as his parents were up at my house celebrating. We had been drinking and somehow we ended up in the bathroom willing each other to have sex. We had no idea what we were doing, neither of us experienced, both virgins. We locked the bathroom door and turned out the light. The wooden bathroom floor was hard and cold. A tiny bathroom mat lay between my back and its harshness. He lay on top of me and entered me without so much as a loving kiss or a tender touch. Up until that point I can't remember feeling anything with such pain. Not one bit how I had imagined sex to be. It was so cold and I felt nothing but pain and embarrassment afterwards. I had no idea that it was normal to bleed after the first time so I got worried. I was in no hurry to repeat it again and certainly not with Sam. When I had refused to repeat the act he had asked me to touch him instead. I did as he asked but I was so uncomfortable about doing so that I said no when he asked again.

When we broke up I found myself crying on Gavin's shoulder. He had a soft side unlike Sam. He hadn't liked the way Sam treated me weeks previous to us splitting. He had used me, got what he wanted but when I refused to repeat that awful night he binned me. He thought he was the man soon surrounding himself with other girls blocking me out, getting stoned all the time and hooking up with girls that would give him what he wanted. Maybe my parents could see that in him all along. I just don't know. He had introduced me to smoking pot and I kind of enjoyed it, enjoyed being in the gang so to speak. Once he had had enough of me it was Gavin that fixed me, made me realise that sex and relationships had more to them. He chose me over his friend and I admired him for that. He stood up for something he believed in even if it meant turning his back on a friendship.

My parents seemed to like this one. He was funny, handsome and pleasant to the unforeseen eye. Together we got up to loads of mischief. He lived at the same end of town as me but went to a different secondary school. He would skive school and set off the fire alarms in school just so that he got to see me at the school gates. His older brother would buy us booze and we would sit in his house getting merry and fumbling about. Sex then wasn't anything near as good as it is now but at the time it was the frill of doing it that was great. I felt comfortable and at ease with Gavin. I wasn't a virgin anymore and I was proud of it, even though orgasms were something that only happened at night, at home in bed alone.

Nothing seemed to bother him when it came to sex. If I had my period he would just tear the pad off and throw it out his bedroom window. I had to walk home with toilet paper between my legs one afternoon as I didn't have a replacement pad in my school bag. Looking back now, I was so shy. I found it refreshing to have someone direct me when it came to sex but did so in a loving manner. I didn't like to strip down in front of anyone, not even in the changing rooms at school. I didn't really believe or had considered what my body was capable of doing. I never did until I met my husband.

Through Gavin I met other people, people who encouraged the bad in me. I started to steal. I had once stolen a cassette from a cousin as I really wanted it and no one would buy me it. I know that was wrong but

I was too young to understand at the time. Now I was a teenager and I grew greedy to a point that if I seen something I liked I had to have it, even if it meant risking a criminal record to get it. It was a thrill, it made me feel alive. Gavin's best friend lived in tall house in the centre of town and being the eldest he had a room on the top floor for his own privacy. We would go out on shop lifting sprees then come back to his house to see what we had all managed to get our hands on. Celebrating became a ritual of sex. We would have sex as couples in the same room often in the same bed. Never sharing or swopping partners but all the same it was a thrill. Four people under the same roof, in the same room, same double bed touching, feeling and having sex. It was like a drug, an addiction.

I became almost unrecognisable. I started stealing out with our little group. At school I got caught stealing and ended up grounded. I started drinking at school, pouring vodka into little bottles of coke and drank it like it was just juice, just anything to help me get through the school day. I felt like a no body at school, hated break times as I would often be found wondering about by myself like a loner. I pushed Gavin away like a used toy. We had had this catchphrase from our favourite movie 'Casper' which was "Can I keep you". Quite catching seeing what happened next. We had been so infatuated with each other then suddenly I was pushing him away for what reason? I don't know. He had been nothing but loving towards me, never said a bad word about me. He was always there for me no matter what but I was feeling suffocated. It took for him to break up with me to realise what I had lost. We got back together but ultimately I got what I deserved when he got offered a sexual act that I wouldn't give him from someone else. I couldn't let him touch me with those hands after they had been on someone else. Not now. I had pushed him too far, there was no way back.

"A mind, stretched to new dimensions by images, thoughts and ideas, can never return to its former shape" _Travis Luedke

Chapter Eight

Kinlochleven was a place of respite for me. It was where I went to forget all the stuff that was going on at home. Summer holidays were longed for and every year I would go to stay with my Aunt and Uncle. No parents, no brother to taunt me. I loved it. I got to know all of my cousin's friends. Like the people back home they also drank, took drugs, enjoyed load music and had sex.

Garry in my eyes was handsome and like other guys I had been interested in, had a passion for music which I found endearing. He made me a mixed tape with all his favourite songs on it. Then one night while babysitting his nephew everyone took their cue and left us alone, he took me to bed and shared with me his knowledge of sex, positions I had never been in before. Who knew I could bend my legs up over his shoulders for deeper penetration, by god I suffered for it afterwards. Everyone said I was walking like I had got off the back of a horse. I grew infatuated by him.

He taught me the importance of contraception. My Mum had put me on the contraceptive pill when I was 15 just months after I met Garry. There was a split condom and a trip to the local doctors for the morning after pill. It made me feel sick so he snuggled me and on a trip out in the car he reached back from the front of the car to rub my leg, smiling at me in the mirror, letting me know he was thinking of me.

Ultimately all holiday romances have to end and this one ended with a gut wrenching feeling in the pit of my stomach as the car drew away and I seen his face disappear as I headed farer away in the opposite direction. I always had a feeling of sadness when I left to go home, when we reached the glens at Glencoe I would zone out and think of all the happy times I had had. This time though I had met someone, he had chased me in his friend's car and Dad had pulled over in a lay-by to let me out and say goodbye to him. I was actually besotted by him and deep down I knew I would probably never see him again. But every school holiday I would go back and hope he is still there. He was gone, he had joined the army.

I would hang out with old friends, get drunk and one night ended up having sex with a friend in the bushes. I got so drunk on another occasion that I passed out. I remember leaning over a bin being sick by the bridge that separated the village into two. The next memory I had was waking up in the toilets of the Masonic Lodge. Some poor person had carried me across the village out cold and my cousin was trying to sober me up. We got found out for drinking that night but the almighty hangover was punishment enough.

I had fallen in love with dance music, longed to go to a proper rave one day. I painted acid men and hash plants on my bedroom wall, scribbled silly drawings and sayings into old school jotters. I was obsessed even though I had not once popped a pill in my life. Well not unless you class a paracetamol. It was yet another phase that eventually faded out, one that my parents must off been glad to see the back off. The music looking back was pretty loud and most of didn't really make any sense but at the time I loved it.

"Getting dragged back into the bad stuff in order for you to learn from your mistakes is a hard lesson to learn – but a solid one." _Mary L Sibbit

Chapter Nine

My cousin Danielle came to live with us, to get away from her little village and to study hairdressing while I continued on at school. We were now both 16 years old and had put our name down with the council for a flat together. We had a close bond, closer than it had ever been while we were younger. It was so nice to have her around as although I had friends in the street to hang out with, at school I was still a loner and I looked forward to nights and weekends being able to spend time together. Sometimes if she wasn't at college she would come meet me at the school gates. It made me feel like I actually had a friend on this earth. We could speak to each other about anything.

She started shop lifting not knowing my past and soon I was dragged back into it, getting caught and taken to the police station with all of her stolen goods in my bag. I didn't say a word to anyone about her involvement as I didn't want to get her into trouble. I can say now that I would never shoplift again. My heart was racing, not knowing what was going to happen to me, locked up in a cell for so long. Not knowing if Danielle had told my parents but also knowing that at 16 the police didn't legally have to get my parents involved. I was accountable for my own actions. But I still had to explain where I had been for the last few hours. The only reason they found out in the end was the envelope addressed to me a few days later stamped from the court. I can safely say I learned my lesson. Luckily it was dropped and I didn't have to face court because of a first offence. I made out I had never done it before but really this was just the 1st time I had got caught and risked any serious punishment.

We started smoking together, trying to hide it from my parents. Saving money and going halves on a ten deck of fags. Waiting until my parents had gone to bed then leaning out my bedroom window for a puff. We would go to under 18's Ballies every Friday night. It was a kid's nightclub where almost every teenager went. We were always tipsy or off our face drunk after drinking White lightening or Merry down either in the toilets at Pleasureland or behind The Seaforth Hotel. Once I fell backwards into the paddling pool down the front, drenched but still I got in. Our bags always got searched but people always managed to sneak stuff in. Drugs were readily available had we wanted them, people in the toilets selling them but we were never interested in them. We just wanted to get drunk, have a dance and be with guys if they were interested.

"Men chase by night those they will not greet by day" _Camille Paglia

It had been a while since we had both lost our virginity so being with guys wasn't unusual. Fueled with alcohol I felt invincible, carefree and in a way confident. If a guy was keen I would have no worry straddling them. We would kiss and touch each other like nobody was looking. When we had had enough Danielle and I would take to the dance floor when our favourite songs would come on.

We weren't the only ones like this on a Friday night. Most teenagers where getting drunk and hooking up with guys but for some reason I felt like I was getting a raw deal. I always seemed to go for the bad eggs, the ones who would either deny being with me or make it out to be something so much more than it was, in the end either making me feel cheap or putting me on a pedestal for their mates to have a go. I had left the club early one night with a guy not realising he had told his mates his intentions to fuck me. The alcohol was starting to wear of so when he asked me to put the condom on him I clammed up and refused to do so. He got a bit frustrated with me and ended up doing it himself, then slammed his frustration into me on the concrete floor. When he was done I realised he had told everyone what he was away to do and where. They had all been watching us from the start. I was made to feel like a whore, while he was the big hero who had scored another notch on his bedpost. I didn't think I was a whore, I was just exploring my sexuality, I was searching for something to fill what seemed to be a gaping hole in my life. I was a teenager going about things in the wrong way. Maybe I should off waited to explore that side of life but in a way I wanted to feel needed by someone. I was looking for love but in all the wrong places.

"It was a mistake, you said. But the cruel thing was, it felt like the mistake was mine, for trusting you" _David Levithan

My first up close encounter with the male penis wasn't what I wanted it to be, resulting in me hating being up close and personal with any guys never regions. It was Hogmany and I wasn't where I said to my parents I was. We had gone to the steeple then back to a guy from schools house for an all night party. Jake's mate was a guy I had come across a few times while out and about. You could say I quite liked him but he had shown no interest in me. We got drunk and had been left alone in Jake's bedroom. To my shock he started kissing me. Then there was the dreaded force full hand placed on the top of your head, sending me south to his now fully erect and waiting penis. I knew what he wanted me to do but I didn't know how to. Even with the alcohol I was scared but not wanting to look like the tease, I did it anyway, made it up as I went along, he reciprocated by asking me to sit on his face. I knew what he wanted to do but I had never had a guy's mouth anywhere near my privates. I did as he asked, sat there until he got fed up, never knew what the fuss was all about. Was I meant to feel anything from it? At the time it all just seemed like pointless sex acts, didn't really do anything for me. The next day he denied being with me and I learnt to my horror that he was in a long term relationship. What had I done? It was no wonder that he wouldn't own up to what had happened. He just looked at me with disgust when his mates teased him about the time we had had alone in that bedroom that night. I was a no body getting nowhere fast.

I carried on at school trying to ignore the taunts from guys and the filthy looks from girls. I poured myself into my studies did anything I could to block them all out. I got myself my first job working in the newsagents Yules. I did all my training in the bigger store at the bottom of the high street later moving up to the one closer to home. I would work from 6am making up the rounds for the paper boys and finish with just enough time to go home for a quick change into my school clothes and head off to school. Some days I would be back down for starting again at 4pm finishing at 8pm on lottery nights. I sometimes got a Saturday shift thrown in which was great seeing that Danielle and I were saving to buy stuff for the flat we had our name down for. For £2 an hour you could say I was being robbed but I loved the extra pennies I was making. I was studying for my exams at the same time and through all my hard work and dedication I got the grades I had hoped for. I wanted to be a graphic designer so had no choice but to stay on at school into 5th year even though I hated it. Art and Graphic Communication were the two highers I chose to study. I had to study several other subjects but none of them really mattered. The only one that I liked out of them was Photography. I learned to develop my own photos and with the subject we were allowed the freedom to exit the school to take pictures of our chosen subjects.

Alfie was in my photography class and Danielle and I had bumped into him and his friends a few times while out and about. Alfie had been in my class in primary 7 at primary school. We had kissed once in the bushes many years ago but I had lost contact with him when we had moved up to secondary. We got to know Alfie and his mates really well, started to hang out together out with school. They were a breath of fresh air after feeling so alone at school for so any years. I always had Alfie to talk too being in the same classes together and we would often walk home together.

Gerry, Alfie's best friend was the one who caught my eye from the start. You could say I fancied him rotten but he wasn't interested in me at first. Danielle was the one he wanted. That was until she left to go back home to Kinlochleven, she had given up her dream to be a hairdresser and decided to go back home. Suddenly I was the lone girl hanging about with a load of guys. But really just because Danielle had left, why should I lose a group of friends just because they were of opposite sex? I trusted every single one of them. I adored them all in my own way, all of different personalities. Even my parents got to know them all. Just like having a big group of brothers.

My desire to be with Gerry hadn't died though. He had left early one night while we were all drinking down the dammy, one of our usual hangouts. I had swallowed a fair bit of cider and a few bottles of beer and started to feel the burning desire down below while mucking about with a couple of the guys, doing silly guy things taunting each other. I wasn't very lady like at the time, was seen as one of the guys, I had been seen that way for some time. I suppose after so long being in a group of friends of the opposite sex they eventually stopped feeling like they were different.

There were three of us left that night and we ended up wandering off towards home, through the woods, fumbling about and taunting each other. One thing led to another then it happened. We kissed. First it was just the one guy then the other joined in. Soon I was on my back one guy with his head between my legs and the other kissing me and groping at my chest. It was a night that was never spoken of again, brushed off like it never happened. But I still remember. I remember feeling alive and wanted, like something had been awoken within me. Suddenly I was being noticed by them almost as if they hadn't realised before that I was female. A few of them that hadn't been there that night had developed a crush on me but I never let anything happen between us. I didn't want to give them false hope of our relationships being anything more than just friendship. I still only had eyes for one guy and I was crying out for him to notice me.

It was during one of our nights out at a friend's house that the teasing started. We had all been drinking when everyone in the room turned around and told us we were made to be together. That was when after all those months of longing to be with him he finally kissed me.

"Just friends, over and over you said it again-then you kissed me"
_Co co. J . Ginger

"After you've seen behind the façade of a stage set you can't take the play seriously anymore. You can't go backwards and regain your ignorance. You have to move forward."   _Zeena Schreck

Chapter Ten

Being a new couple was so fresh and exciting. I started to feel like I was someone again. I had a purpose. Being one of those couples that everyone knew was suddenly what I was known for. All loved up and full of fun. I no longer felt like the little slut crying out for attention. I was in a proper relationship now.

My parents had known Gerry for a while so when we ended up together they were great about it. You see Gerry had this charm about him. All adults adored him. Old grannies would smile at him when he spoke kindly to them and he was always willing to help them with carrying shopping, walking them across the road and the likes. He had manners of a guy I had never come across before. He was like a knight in shining armour. I was the rescued princess being saved from her past.

He had a passion for music. Playing his guitar, writing songs and the sound he made from his harmonica. I loved all of it. I would sit for hours just watching and dreaming him in. He played the drums in a band but the guitar was his instrument of choice. He would spend hours playing either his acoustic guitar or whenever the house was empty he would be on the electric guitar with the amp blasting out. Our friend Geoffrey played too and often they would jam together. He once tried to teach me how to play a Nirvana song but I was nowhere near as good as him. He liked to write songs and had once written a song for my cousin Danielle. I never understood why he wrote one for her and not me. He loved Oasis and through listening to him play I grew to like new genres of music. If I didn't have my Nirvana unplugged cd on it would be one of my many Oasis ones.

The sex was great, well to me at that point I hadn't had proper loved up sex before. It was different and exciting. I felt comfortable with him.

I didn't feel ashamed or felt that certain expectations were expected of me. Gerry had been a virgin when we first got together and I found it kind of cool guiding him, breaking him in gently so to speak. We started to get more experimental the more we did it and the more comfortable we became with each other. Being naked in front of my partner was never an issue then. We weren't ashamed of our selves or our sex life, often being unable to control our self 's, having sex right under our friend's noses, under the covers as they looked on watching whatever was on the tv at the time or playing video games. We would have foreplay before sex which I had never done before. It had always been either just sex or just foreplay. Although I wasn't entirely comfortable going down on him it wasn't because I didn't like to see his penis but because I really didn't know what I was doing. I once drew his privates while he posed for me as a study when I was at college studying art. I had been doing nude drawing and he wanted me to draw him. We just weren't shy about our nakedness which was a great thing to have.

My parents after much discussion decided to start letting him stay over, their little girl was growing up. Mum had put me on the contraceptive pill when I was 15 years old so I guess they suspected I was ready long before I got with Gerry.

Being a couple changed the dynamics of our wee group. Mum and Dad had gotten to know everyone. They would come over and we would all hang out in the converted attic room or in mine or Dylan's bedroom. They had even helped to dig out Mum and Dad's new driveway. With the new dynamics there were fewer of us. Friends drifted off and made new friends, apart from a certain few who had been close friends of Gerry's for years. We all would hang out together playing computer games, drinking, fooling around having a laugh. We would study together, usually me studying and Gerry playing his guitar. We skived school together, had meals together and slept together at night. The only difference from an adult relationship was that we both lived at home with our parents. He would be up early for his paper round every day, would then nip home for a change then meeting up with me before school registration. At weekends Dad would have made him a fry up breakfast ready for him coming back from his Sunday paperbound as he didn't need to go home after his shift.

In the beginning I had still been working at the newsagents. Gerry would sometimes come and meet me on the weekends when I was due my lunch break. I couldn't wait to get my shift over with so that I could be with him. I was just so loved up. My world began and ended with him. A few months after getting the job I hurt my back trying to pick up a crate of juice cans and ended up signed off my work and school for 5 months. I was in so much pain at the time, constantly popping pills and eventually getting an appointment to see a physiotherapist who gave me a load of exercises which even to this day I follow if it flares up.

In the end I had to give up my job with being off so long. I was now studying for my Highers which I found really difficult as I had missed so much of school. The artwork and design work was easy enough as I could do that at home. I even managed to study for my art history exam acing every part of all the exams apart from the technical drawing side of my graphic communication exam. I had all A's but ended up with a fail in my Higher Graphic com exam due to not having the confidence and knowledge to finish the exam to the ability that I knew I had. Having no teacher to show and explain the work to me was my down fall. I was so disappointed at the time. I did get the opportunity to re-sit the exam the following year while I was at college studying Art and Design which to begin with I did study for but I found it hard. I was doing a full time Art and design course and I had started doing my Higher English and Higher Psychology at night school. In the end I gave up and concentrated on my English as I knew it was going to be really hard for me to pass with it being one of two subjects at school that I struggled in, the second being Maths.

I do truly believe Gerry was my first proper love. Discovering these feelings made me realise that everything before was just infatuation, teenage crushes. Like most relationships at that age. It came to an end. I was distraught when it ended, couldn't believe I was now alone. We had been together for so long, had barely spent a day without seeing each other or at least speaking to one another. Things between us had got harsh towards the end but I loved him. I truly believe that if it wasn't for this relationship with all its ups and downs, I wouldn't off been capable of loving my husband today. I learned what it was like to be in a proper relationship and what not to do when things got rough.

I started college and loved it, loved being around so many new faces and learning so many new things, things that I was keen to learn. I longed to be a graphic designer. Gerry on the other hand had left school and got a job, had no passion other than his music. He got a job as a labourer with my next door neighbour. I was really chuffed for him at first but his boss was a bit of a prick. He was a womaniser and he would tease me, planted seeds in my mind about Gerry's whereabouts when they were out at work. Later he became a waiter at a local restaurant and would be working till the early hours of the morning. When he could he would be out doing gigs so we didn't see as much of each other as we had before. I started to get jealous of other girls being near my man, started to lose my trust in him because he didn't feel close anymore. I had gone up north to visit family and he couldn't come so he house sat for us. When we returned I found kirby grips in my room and in my bed. Had he brought someone back to the house, to the bed that we shared? To this day I still don't know. He swore he wasn't playing away but by this point I had become so jealous of his lack of interest for me and his ongoing nights away that we were broken. He started to get nasty towards me would always be throwing some harsh comment my way. My arse would block out the sun was the one that always stuck in my mind and hurts even today thinking how horrible he had become towards me.

"Insanity is doing the same thing over and over again but expecting different results"

The constant arguments were like this huge weight crushing me. I wanted to break free but didn't know how to fix it all. Sex became unwanted, unneeded. I would lie back and just let him get on with it. No pleasure, no tenderness. When he was about he was either drinking ignoring me or spending time in the room next door playing computer games with my brother. No attention left for me in this sorry excuse for a relationship. He would often come back through at bedtime and climb into bed and expect us to have sex. I got so fed up with it, would pretended to be asleep. He would still spread my legs apart and thrust himself in me even when I pretended to snore. On two occasions I can remember sitting on the edge of the bed and we had started to argue, he was drunk and punched me. The first time it was on the right arm, second time square on the cheek. I had never been hit like that before and it had been by the person I was in love with. He was pushing me to the edge almost as if he wanted the relationship to end but couldn't be man enough to just end it himself. He just had to push and push until I snapped. When I did, it didn't last long. Just couldn't be without him. All I had known for the last two years was over. We ended back together always me running back to him. Then he didn't phone or come and see me on my 18th birthday. That was it, the last straw. I realised that day that no matter how gut wrenching it was, I had to break free. It was killing my parents seeing me so upset. They loved him but hated what he was doing to me. What he had reduced me to. So on the night of my 18th, I wasn't out celebrating with my family and friends. I was putting an end to all that I had relied on for the last two years. I was setting us both free,

free to grow and explore again, a decision that changed my life forever.

At the time I couldn't see a light at the end of the tunnel. I had a good friend in a girl called Charlotte, she was a friend from college but we would hang out at weekends. Charlotte lived in Dundee but was learning to drive, would drive through in her mum's car. She was there for me after Gerry and I split. She stayed over the weekend of my 18th birthday, brought me a lovely bottle of wine with a Koala bear stamped on the front. It had meaning because she knew how much I loved Koalas and longed to visit Australia. We ate junk, watched silly movies, I cried and she was there to pick me up.

I poured myself into my studies at college, spent more time with friends. I could now go to pubs and clubs and drink as much as I wanted. Stay out late and even stay over with friends from out of town. I was introduced to the culture of getting blind drink, legally. Friends shared the same passion I had for art and it made me feel like I belonged. I was no longer at school surrounded by people who didn't understand me and my interests. I still thought about him but really it was the idea of having someone to snuggle into, someone to lay bare with. I missed it so god dam much. I wanted to forget, become someone else. People from my past looking at me like a failure, the failed relationship. We were so well known as a couple and now we were single. Shortly after we broke up I made a spur of the moment decision to go to the hairdressers one lunch time. No one recognised me as I walked back into the painting studio. I no longer had long brunette waves of hair but short scrunched up to look curly hair just above the shoulder, in shock blonde. Looking back at pictures I really don't know what I was thinking but it helped. It made me feel like someone else, the new young carefree me.

With my new found college friends we began to feel a bit like a wee family, a mad family but never the less a family. We would spend afternoons off in the West port bar, lining up shots and having a carry on. Some nights we would house sit while Archie's parents were away. We introduced Maisie to Hooch there one night resulting in her topping a sofa chair and me looking after her as she puked her guts up in Archies's toilet, saving her hair clasp from being flushed down the toilet by reaching in for it. The Student Union in Dundee was visited on numerous weekends by Charlotte and I, cheap double vodkas and lemonades resulted in a hangover to top any illness I'd ever had in my life, having to go home early as I actually looked green.

College days consisted of a packet of Mexican Mccoys and a cream egg at break time, Chips with cheese and mayo at lunch and a whole load of sexual innuendo in between. There was always playful banter and teasing going on in class. I knew that Archie had an apparent crush on me but I just saw him as a good friend. I never liked to encourage any guy who had an unwanted crush on me and there had been a lot over the years. From a guy called Jt at school who would always try to give me teddies and love notes to two good friends of Gerry and I's. Alfie and Mason backed off when Gerry and I got serious but were still hanging about trying to be seen when we broke up.

At college Patrick, Mia, Maisie and Archie would sometimes tease me about a guy called Mathew from our class who liked me when we first started college but I was with Gerry and brushed it off, believed Mathew to be in a relationship and there to be no truth to the teases. Once Gerry and I split I was free to party, one of them at an overnight party at Mathew's house in Montrose. The guys were still teasing me about Mathew at this point. I was single now but really hurting inside. Mathew was now attached so even if I had been in the right frame of mind, it couldn't off happened. Years later I found out that he did like me back then but it obviously wasn't meant to be. I will always see him as the one that fell through the cracks, a great guy not so dissimilar to me, similar in a way that only he will understand.

College was a great place to be, surrounded by great people. A moment in time that yes, I would go back and do it all again, possibly this time starting off without the troubles I faced at home with Gerry and for definitely making a better effort to keep in touch with everyone after we left.

"I may not have gone where I intended to go, but I think I have ended up where I needed to be" _Douglas Adams

A lot changed in me in the coming months. Not just my new look but I was starting to grow tired. I was starting to lose my passion for what I had studied for the last 6 years. I had been so certain of what I wanted to become and now nothing was clear anymore. A letter arrived from University to say I hadn't been accepted. There were over 700 applicants for only 140 spaces. That was it I just didn't want to do it anymore. I couldn't take the knock back. I felt rejected and dealt with it the only way I knew how. I tried to reinvent myself by doing something different. But what was I going to do with my life?

I was working weekends at this point in a local factory and loved the extra money it was giving me. I would work a 12 hr night shift on a Friday night then do a 12 hour day shift on a Sunday leaving the week days for my studies. I couldn't stop my studies all together but what was I going to do? I think in the end it was a case of opening the college brochure and picking out whatever appealed, something that I had never considered before, Beauty therapy. To everyone's shock, I applied. I had always been very tom boyish, never wore make up, always in sweatpants and trainers. I got accepted and a new chapter began. College came to an end and we decided to leave on a high note by having a night out in Dundee. Mia stayed in Dundee so we all decided to bunk down at her parent's house. During the day in Dundee before we all got ready to go out we had gone down town shopping and I decided to get my belly button pierced, a rash decision that ended up with us in the pub next door for a glass of water and Maisie and Mia having to guide me to the toilet as my eye sight went black, just seconds before I passed out in the corridor to the toilets. By god it hurt but it was our last night out before we all went our separate ways and I couldn't let it spoil the night. We had a meal followed by a pub crawl and partying in one of Dundee's many nightclubs. It was sad to say good bye the next morning, was the last time I was to see most of my college friends. Thankfully due to modern technology I can now speak to a small few that I've managed to look up. It's not the same though, so many years between then and now has distanced us, broken the wee family we once had but I will always cherish our time together at college.

I continued to work, taking all the extra shifts I could get at the factory. I had been working weekends up until the summer and was now able to do the extra shifts. I needed the money now to pay the college fees for the next term.

With it now being the summer Kinlochleven was on the cards. I met a guy called Declan, a friend of my cousin Danielle's. I liked him instantly, his tan and his cheeky lip. It was time for me to start rebuilding myself, time to move on from Gerry. Declan was on crutches, had his leg wrapped up in plaster following a car crash. Mason, Gerry and I's mutual friend and I had a caravan to our self, was meant to be a group of us going but I had my suspicions that Gerry had put them off the idea. I'm sure the only reason that Mason still came was because he still had that crush on me from school, he was after all Gerry's best friend so why else would he come? Maybe I was just too suspicious but I had reason to be. From the day Gerry and I had split up I had been receiving nuisance calls. Sometimes there would just be no one on the other end but on other occasions they would play the song 'Do you believe in life after love' by Cher. It was really weird and it had fucked with my brain.

On the holiday we had parties and lots of them. During one of them a local guy that I didn't know had turned up. At first I didn't mind him being there until he got all weird when I asked him to take his drugs outside. I didn't want him smoking pot in the caravan and certainly didn't want any other drug type associated with me either. He wouldn't leave us alone even after we locked him out and told him to clear off. My cousin Mick and his friend Aaron chased him away with a metal pole.

Danielle and I teased the guys, encouraged them to strip tease for us, and they did. What a laugh that night, even my Mum and Aunty came for a drink to get away from their husbands in the caravan at the other end of the park. Declan must off seen something in me that night while we partied. We ended up in bed with each other after the adults left. Danielle, Mick her younger brother, Aaron Declan's friend and Mason teased us that night while we had sex in the twin bedroom. Coming in and switching on and off the lights and giggling listening to us and laughing at the caravan rocking. With him being crippled I had to sit on top of him, having sex for hours with sweat pouring off us. We were young, drunk and didn't care. Secretly I think Mason was distraught as he knew there was no chance of anything between us with Declan about and us having had sex. To be honest I didn't really care, I had put up with enough shit from his best friend. I feel bad for him now looking back. I was a bit of a bitch for doing that to him. Maybe he truly was just trying to be a friend.

The holidays were over and it was a new term at college and a brand new course for me to get to grips with. Keira had moved up from Liverpool and that first night in the beauty room we instantly clicked, she was loud, mouthy. Full of life and just what I needed. Drinking was a pastime at weekends and drinking a whole bottle of whiskey between us with coke was normal. She had a second living room that we would always claim, would stay up late making silly videos of ourselves for fun. She stole her mums car once, no license, just didn't care. Her mum and step dad to this day always speak. Demi, Keira's mum was like no other friends mum I had met at the point, a great laugh. She was like one of the girls.

We got our tattoos around the same time, around the time of my 19th birthday. We went out to celebrate with friends and were showing them off in The Westport Bar. Keira had gotten a wee devil on her right shoulder blade and I decided on a blue rose with a tribal design through, it also on my right shoulder blade. My cousin Danielle had been with me when I got mine in Dundee and had gotten a Chinese symbol, something to represent the baby she had lost not long before she came to visit. Just like when I got my belly button pierced I passed out. This time I ended up with bruises on the tops of my arms from where the tattooist had had to hold me up when I went limp. He was great about it, told us stories of grown men, some bikers that had passed out while getting tattoos. I felt great having had a tattoo, wanted to show it off all the time.

Holidays would come again and I would go back, always ending back in bed with him. Declan was the sort of guy that liked his fun, was a bit of a player. Looking back he played me so well, kept me coming back for more. He told me one drunken night that he was going to marry me when we were older, this didn't help the situation as I grew infatuated with him. Back home I would phone him, sometimes he was around and other times he was avoiding me. I knew that but like a moth to a flame I couldn't stay away. His mate asked me one night for something, I had no idea what it was. I felt like a silly little girl until they explained. The two of them wanted a spit roast, two men inside me at once. Now with all that I have experienced its one of those things I would have loved to have done, something that can only be simulated while using toys with my husband. I refused of course but really I wish I had done it, to say I had experienced it. The one and only time offer that never happened. I was young and scared, hadn't experimented much with sex, I hadn't wandered too far from the norm.

He stayed over one night at my parent's holiday home. We had sex on the couch a few times that night. The frill of getting caught was too over powering to say no. I'm sure my Dad had seen us through the glass topped door while getting up for the toilet, I'm sure because he wasn't about when we got up, had gone fishing early and stayed away all day. He couldn't look me in the eye when he came home. I felt like I had let him down. My whole life my Dad had been my hero, to me he was ten feet tall. He had to let me go. I wasn't a little girl anymore. I know he was just looking out for me. As a parent, I know that now, but that feeling inside was and always will be worse than any punishment a parent can lash out, the feeling of guilt and the sense that someone who loves you being ashamed of you. The silence alone could hurt a thousand men.

Keira had got herself a good guy by now and I started to see her less and less. She was all loved up and I felt lonely. They were really good with me even though most of the time I felt like a spare part. They took me to Dundee once after I told Keira some of the stuff I remembered about living there, being so confident she walked straight up to the door of one of my old friends and asked for Steven. To my shock he still lived there but the funny thing was that he wasn't in but his mum said she would tell him that she had been for him. She even left her real name. I would off loved to be a fly on the wall when he got the message.

My cousin Danielle had come down for the weekend and we had arranged to meet up with a few of our old friends, among them was Gerry. We hadn't really spoken since we broke up but suddenly I craved him again, well I thought I did. It wasn't him I wanted It was a man of my own. I wanted to be loved up just like Keira, wanted to be in a proper relationship again. That night after Gerry had left, I felt gutted, gutted that nothing had happened between us. I began drinking more, dancing, dancing to let off steam. Then a guy approached me, asked for my number, nothing else. No conversation, no cheesy chat up lines, no attempt at a grope. He didn't even ask me back to the party he was heading to, Just a smile of acknowledgement and a peck on the lips as he left. One single peck that changed everything forever, the acknowledgement that ultimately resulted in everything I know today, a kiss that resulted in a love that no man could even remotely measure up to.

"The seeker embarks on a journey to find what he wants and discovers, along the way, what he needs"   _Wally Lamb

"Sometimes our light goes out, but it is blown again into flame by an encounter with another human being each of us owes the deepest thanks to those who have rekindled this inner light"   _Albert Schweitzer

Chapter Eleven

Friday the 29th September 2000 was the date, the day when I met my soul mate for the first time. He swept in that night and saved me from a path of desperation. I had so desperately wanted to get back with Gerry that night and he walked away leaving me feeling even more empty and foolish for even thinking there was still something there. Back to drinking with the rest of the gang, I couldn't let Danielle down. She had come down to visit for the weekend and was out for a good night. I still remember what I was wearing that night, a grey pair of skrousers, white top and hair tied back in one of those awful scrunchies that looked like hair with purple and blue strands coming out of it.

I was dancing away getting drunk with Danielle as everyone had spread out and disappeared from our radar when a guy approached me and asked me for my number. That was all, just a number, gave me a quick peck on the lips and said he would call. Then he was gone.

It was Saturday afternoon and for some odd reason that I can't quite remember, Gerry had turned up on my door step to see me and Danielle. He had got roped into helping Dad shift a shed in the back garden and that's when he called. At first I was a taken back and didn't know what to say. He wanted to meet up but I brushed him off. Danielle was only down for one more night and I didn't want to ditch her to meet up with some guy I didn't know. I had the old guy in my back garden using his charm to win over my Dad and I had the new guy on the phone all dark, dangerous and completely brand new. I knew what I had to do and it wasn't brush this new guy off completely, I had to get rid of the old.

I had recently bought myself my first mobile phone, a Vodafone, with that I could now speak in privacy to my friends and not have to cart the house phone through to my bedroom from the living room.

We spoke on the phone everyday for at least a week before we finally met face to face for the first time. I learned he was a lorry driver who was 26 to my 19 years of age. Wow an older guy, I'd always wanted to know what it was like to be with an older guy. I got butterflies in my stomach every night waiting for the call. I felt terrible about it but I had no idea of what he actually looked like. The night when we met it was dark in the dingy nightclub and I was fuelled with alcopops. I fell for the man behind the phone. A guy I learned to laugh with, to share my stories with like a best friend but had never properly met. We arranged to meet the following weekend after work.

I was filled with excitement and nerves all day during my shift at Focus. I hadn't really been working there long but at the time I loved my job. He had told me he would pick me up in his little silver car, a Renault Megane. I had no idea what the car looked like as I was no car buff and I had no idea what he looked like either. It was dark outside and I remember signing out at the reception desk and thinking, omg what was I doing???

The car park was almost empty apart from the odd cars bellowing to staff ending their shift like myself. He was standing there against this sporty looking number. Tall, dark haired and oh my god I bagged myself an actual guy who by the looks of it looked after himself and must have cash to drive a car like that. I had never gone out with a guy with a car before so it was all so exciting and fresh. Of course I wasn't really bothered whether he had money or not as none of my previous boyfriends had had what you would call a luxurious life style and nor had I. I was nervous and was happy that we had finally met face to face for the first time.

We went for a drive and ended parked up at the sea front facing out to the sea. We talked for hours, talking about everything and anything, having a laugh and enjoying each other's company. His surname was Sibbit. I had asked him repeatedly what it was but he wouldn't tell me. I eventually got it out of him. Still to this day I don't know why he was so embarrassed to tell me. It couldn't be as weird as mine, Croll. Id grown up being called a crow and it really pissed me off. Mark Sibbit a man of many mysteries but they were going to be mine to discover. With the stars and moon twinkling above us and the sea crashing in front it was the first night of many more to come.

My parents were quite annoyed the next day when they found out I had been out till the early hours of the morning with some guy I had just met. How old is he? What does he do? The third degree… great!! I knew they were concerned when I told them he was much older and a truck driver but they had to let me choose for myself.

Sunday following our Friday night face to face and Mark had arranged to pick me up from the house and take me out for the day. He waited in the car outside for me, too soon to meet the parents but it would come soon enough. It was a lovely sunny day and I was filled with excitement. We drove and talked for hours, ended up going cross country to Aberdeen. His passion was trucks which I didn't really understand. He was so different from the guys I had dated before. Almost every one of them had a passion for music in some form or another but Mark was different and it intrigued me.

We went to Burger king for something to eat but I only had fries and a drink. I didn't want him to see me wolfing down a burger so I just nibbled on my fries and watched him eat his. I remember looking at his hands for the first time and thinking, my god his hands are bloody huge! A crazy thought I know but I don't know why, I was probably just nervous of where this was all going, trying to find some sort of fault that wasn't actually there. I must be due to wake up sometime soon and see that this was all just an act. He took me to see 'Hollow man' at the cinema that day and drove me home, kissed me good bye and went home, everything so perfect, my heart swelling for him.

Over the coming weeks and months we continued to meet up and catch up over the phone. He was away a lot being a lorry driver but when he was home he was almost always with me. We met the parents and became a normal couple, trying to spend every waking moment we could with each other. I remember the first time walking into his parent's house and being very shy. It was like walking into my grandparent's house, the décor being old fashioned and there being clutter all over the walls, pictures everywhere. They were very welcoming and loved my name. Marks grandmother on his dad's side was called Mary and they loved the fact that I bared the same name. I actually have the full name now being married.

He would stay over every night that he could and would often bump into my Dad early morning for a coffee before he headed off for his shift. The only time we ever slept together in his parent's house was when I had finished my shift at Focus knowing that Mark was off work ill. I had gone over after a quick change at home and was allowed to go see him in bed. His parents had gone out shopping and we snuggled up in bed watching a film. Spooning as you know usually ends up in forking and certainly did on this occasion. I didn't stay the night though, there was no way his parents would allow it, were a completely different generation from my parents. I was the oldest sibling in my family and Mark the youngest in his. When we both got the chance we would book into hotels nearby so that we could be completely alone. We could do as we wished and didn't have to worry about being heard or walked in on while having sex. I think we tried nearly every Travel Inn within a 30 mile radius. We could bath together, chill out naked together watching crap tv and would order take away. When we weren't together he was still with me, I would day dream about him. If I happened to see him pass my work in his truck while out on a fag break he would blast his horn and wave, making my knees weak, my heart melt and sent the butterflies in my stomach on a frenzie. I was head over heels in love with him and couldn't imagine life being any better.

I had prior to meeting Mark booked a caravan holiday up north to see Danielle but of course now that I was loved up and didn't want to go. The original plan was to go up and party, hook up with guys and have fun. I didn't want to leave Mark and I certainly had no intention to party and hook up with guys. I was going to be travelling up with Mum and Dad as they had their own caravan at the same time but Mark came to my rescue. I was booked in for the week and Mark had the weekends off to take me up and stay a night or two. We drove up all excited getting to spend some quality time together forgetting that Danielle would be at the other end. I loved spending time with Danielle but I loved my new man more. The First night Danielle stayed and we chilled out just the three of us. It was fine but I longed for some alone time with my man. I didn't really like her being around as I was always a little jealous of her after her catching the eye of Gerry first. I didn't want her catching the eye of my new man.

The following day we told Danielle we wanted some time alone and I remember her not being too pleased. I finally had my man to myself and boy did we make use of the caravan. In the bed we went for hours, at the window while I was doing the dishes and in the living room in front of the fire. It was really stormy outside and stuff was flying about everywhere. The power had gone out so there was nothing better to do than go to bed and make the most of our night together. The Sunday he had to leave to go back home for work he left it as late as he possibly could so not to miss a moment with each other. We both had tears in our eyes that night. Even thinking about it now I feel a lump in my throat. I pined for him all week and every time our favourite song came on the radio I would well up, Deleriums 'Silence'. I had to buy it on cd and made everyone in the car coming back from Fort William listen to it over and over. I sent him a post card and a naughty letter in an envelope so that his mum couldn't read it, telling him how much I loved him and what I wanted him to do to me when I saw him next.

Then the weekend came again and he was back. He drove all the way back to get me and take me home. But not before spending one more night alone before we had to go back to reality and our parents houses.

During our first Christmas and I felt tortured to have to spend the day without him. We spent the day with family and had planned for him to come over after his meal. He turned up late and had been drinking with friends resulting in our first argument. It was soon forgotten though and he spent the night making it up to me. We wanted to be together as much as we possibly could but I realised that we were both entitled to time apart with our friends, something I had learnt from my relationship with Gerry.

" To love someone is nothing. To be loved by someone is something. But to be loved by the one you love.......is everything"   _Bill Russell

Chapter Twelve

Our first Valentines and we had previously spoken about getting engaged. We had already started looking into moving in together so I suppose it was bound to happen at some point, it felt right. Mark was away with work on our first Valentines so we celebrated on the 15th. He came over with a lovely bunch of roses and a wee ring box. I didn't know I was actually getting an engagement ring so when I opened the box and seen a diamond ring I couldn't help but smile. I remember feeling so nervous and so happy all at the same time. Was this it? Were we getting engaged? When he didn't get down on one knee like in the movies I wasn't sure what to do so I asked him what finger it was for. Could I put it on my wedding finger? He told me that if it was what I really wanted then yes, yes we were getting engaged. It wasn't the most romantic proposal but I had never been this close to anyone before and it felt so right. Of course I've never let him forget his proposal, he knows I would love him to do it right some day.

We continued to look into having our own space but renting was proving to be very expensive. We both worked full time but I was still at college part time studying beauty care and had fees to pay. Getting a mortgage seemed to be the best investment so we opted to go down that route. After a lot of appointments, saving and house hunting, we finally got the keys to our first home on the 29th June 2001. It was less than a year since we had first met and I suppose to outsiders it would of looked like things were moving way too fast but to us it wasn't. There was never any pressure to do anything or make any of the decisions we did. It all felt so right inside, both my heart and my head at the same time just knew somehow that it was meant to be that way. Luckily I had already started buying household items from when

I was 16 after putting my name on the council housing list with my cousin so it was mainly the big items we had to fork out for.

We had our own wee two bedroom flat just around the corner from his parents house. It was so exciting and I was so wrapped up with the moving and decorating to notice how upset my parents were that I was flying the nest. It was late at night of our last night living with our parents and I was still painting our new living room when I got a phone call from a very upset mother wanting to spent some time with her daughter on her last night at home. I felt awful, I was so wrapped up in my happiness to realise how much Id be missed.

"The best teachers are those who show you where to look, but don't tell you what to see" _Alexandra K.Trenfor

My mum had been so brilliant with everything. Growing up we weren't close. With Mum always working, the things that happened in Dundee then me suddenly becoming a teenager, there hadn't been a lot of time for mother daughter bonding. We still had our moments though. When Gerry and I had got close it was Mum that persuaded Dad to allow him to stay over, when I first told my parents that I smoked it was Mum I turned too and when she knew I was drinking she even allowed me to do it in the house where she could keep an eye on me. I had a lot of respect for parents and the way they brought me up. My Mum had always been there in the background as my guiding support and I can only imagine how she must off felt when her only daughter was leaving.

It was great having our own place. Eating what we could prepare ourselves for meals, lounging on our own couch, sex whenever and wherever we wanted, parties. I was suddenly able to cook what I wanted and started to love it. I had baked the odd cake with my Gran when younger and made the odd dish at school in Home Economics but now I could make stuff that I'd always wanted to try. Back home I would usually eat in my bedroom and when it was something I didn't like I would wrap it up and put it in my bin. I grew to hate Dad's chicken casserole but loved his homemade macaroni. I still make his recipe today but sometimes spice it up a bit by adding something different. I wasn't ill or anything, I didn't have an eating disorder I simply binned anything I didn't want and scoffed everything I loved. Spicy food became a favourite and still is. Curry both Indian and Chinese, Mexican foods like chilli, burritos and tacos were a favourite and Jalapeno chillies, well Mark would eat them raw all the time. The kebab shop down the road loved us at the weekends, a donner kebab for me and a chicken and donner for Mark.

We had a lot to learn about being so independent but we were learning as we went and we loved it. We got comfortable with each other and that's when I started to pile on the pounds. I went from and size 12 to a 14 and remember bumping into Megan in the street and her asking what I had just bought from the clothes shop. I was so embarrassed with the size on the tag and tried to hide it from her. I had never had any bother with my weight before as I had always been slim and was always teased for it when younger, "skinny malinky Mary" was what I got called from my Uncle and some of dads friends. This was the starting point of a long ongoing need to look different, a need to change my body. I had never had any bother getting naked in front of Mark but I was still very shy and didn't realise by how much until now looking back.

It was a good while after Mark and I got together that I finally met his best friend Dillan. We had gone to pick him up after his shift at The Red Lion Caravan Park that first night and I remember feeling a bit nervous. He soon put my mind at rest turning out to be a very cheeky easy going guy. Whenever we had any form of party at the flat Dillan was always in for a laugh. Gerald Marks other friend, the one that had been with him the very first night we met was also around a lot but I didn't click with him. He would always tease Mark telling him I was his ball and chain and trying to get him to go out partying. It's not that I didn't trust Mark I didn't trust his friend. He was Marks friend and had been for a long time so I just tried to see the good in him and would bite my tongue. Mark knew though, he would always be the centre of any arguments caused between us. Gerald had come up with us to Kinlochleven once when my cousin Danielle had got her own place, had met her younger sister Holly and started a thing with her. Mark and Gerald were right into their petrol remote control cars and would take them out and race them. On one occasion in Kinlochleven they were racing them up and down Danielle's street when her neighbour upstairs started going mental. He was a known junkie but had a child inside sleeping, I could see his point and they were pretty loud.

Gerald and Mark had arranged to go to Silverstone for the weekend and I didn't feel good about it, the way Gerald was going on about the fun they would have, kept going on about all the hot chickies at the Grand Prix. Mark was a keen fan of F1 at the time and would watch it on Sunday afternoons when it was in season. They left for the bus that morning after a huge argument between Mark and I. I felt awful, I had to let him do his own thing and I had to trust him. I had to learn from past mistakes.

The fun we had between moving in together and deciding to start a family was like nothing I had ever experienced before. We were young and loved our house parties. Getting drunk, getting stoned and having loads of sex. Mark loved the idea of trying anal sex but I wasn't convinced, got drunk one night and thought fuck it. We didn't really know much about it apart from what we had watched on the porn dvd's .I liked to watch them with him, felt turned on by it. Let's just say that it wasn't successful. It was so painful and nothing like in the dvd's we had seen. I felt so ashamed when I had to make him stop what he was doing, I had an over whelming urge to go to the toilet so locked myself in the bathroom trying to get my head around what had just happened.

It didn't seem to bother Mark though as he would make it known that he still wanted to give it another go. I would just brush it off and tell him I wasn't up for it but really I was dying for it to be like in the dvd's.

When I could I would travel with Mark where ever his job would take him. Sometimes it would only be back and forth to Glasgow delivering potatoes to Alan Bartlets but on a few occasions we would go down south, Newcastle to the breweries with grain and down near London with potatoes. On these long haul trips we would share his single bed inside his truck and sex was always on the cards. I loved to watch him drive, watch him shifting gears. I don't know what it was but watching his arm bulge and his veins pop as he shifted gears turned me on, still does. I loved it when we were in the car together, he would place his left hand on my thigh when he was driving and only shift it to change gear. In the truck he couldn't do that because of the distance between our seats but I would watch from afar and long for his hand on my thigh. The first time I heard him speak on his Cb in the truck I was taken aback, couldn't understand a damn word he was saying. It was like a different language only I seemed to be the only one that didn't understand, truckers language I call it. Jack one of Marks work mates became a good friend of ours would always be getting the crack over the cb. He was older probably ages with my Dad possibly a little older but he was a great laugh, so down to earth and funny. He was a family man and before long I was introduced to his wife and we hit it off instantly, just as mad as her husband.

We went on our first proper holiday together to Blackpool. I had called and booked from an ad in The News of the World and couldn't wait. When we arrived I couldn't off been more disappointed. The hotel was definitely on the shore front as advertised but the likeness stopped there. The whole place was filthy, had children sweeping the hall ways with a dust pan and brush, no hoover in site and the rooms were disgusting. The en-suite was a dingy cupboard with tiles all cracked and a toilet in the shower with a broken sliding door. The window was covered with bars and looked out to the bins at the back of the building. The bed was stained and cob webs hung from the ceiling, the walls would rattle from the couple having sex next door. It was like something out of a New York movie when they end up in a crack whore hotel, the only thing missing was the sirens outside and the screeching cat in the alley way. The only consolation was that we had plenty of weed to get stoned and forget where we had to sleep. It was Illumination time so everything was opened late and buzzing. We would get up early and have breakfast in a nearby café as there was no way in hell I was eating back at the hotel. We spent the day exploring and would stay out really late come back to the hotel and get stoned. We had recently bought our first video camera and got loads of great stuff on it including an amazing firework display. We even videoed the hotel room as we didn't think people would believe how bad it was. I wish we still had the video but we stupidly recorded over it after a drunken night in the pub. We had been out partying and had come home frisky and decided to make a home movie. Being drunk we didn't check to see what the video in the camera was. Let's just say that when looking for the video labelled Blackpool holiday I wasn't expecting to see us both going at it, naked and in a drunken manner. Funny looking back now but at the time I was devastated that we had lost our first holiday video.

"And sometimes it hits me out of nowhere. All of a sudden this overwhelming sadness rushes over me. And I get discouraged and I get upset and I feel hopeless, sad and hurt. And once again, I feel numb to the world."

Chapter Thirteen

We had been living in our own wee bubble for almost a year when we started talking about the possibility of having children. We joked about it at first, about having a wee boy called Jack, then we got serious and I came off the pill on the 10th July 2002 just over a year since we had moved in together. Sex started to become more of a ritual than a spur of the moment thing and really it didn't bother me. What did bother me was the constant disappointment each month when I got my period. Things at work started to go downhill and I was suddenly not happy anymore.

I was doing really well at work, I had been employed as a customer service assistant in the art department in our local Focus store and our department was rated one of the best in Scotland. We would do demonstrations with the products to show the customers how to use them, would run competitions for the kids and I loved my job. Stocking all these different arts and craft products opened my eyes to new crafts. I learned to flower arrange under the supervision of my supervisor Julia. She showed me how to paint on glass, paint on fabrics such as silk and I learned loads about suppliers and that there was a whole other world of arts and crafts out there to explore compared to what I had learned from college. I would come into work every day eager to get started, to get stuck into the thick of it. Even stock checks didn't bother me, the long hours doing overtime, it was the products that interested me and I got on great with most of my co workers, was able to have a laugh. On one occasion we had gotten a delivery of cushion fillers and there must have been about two cages full of the stuff. The shop was empty as it was later on at night and almost closing when a few of us decided to empty the cages up one of the back isles in our department. We would run and dive into the stock like silly children. I miss those days, having companions like that at work, having a carry on and a laugh. Although I love my job today, it can be a very lonely one at times.

Other departments within the store started to go downhill, weren't getting the ratings that we were getting in the art department. We were made to help out more in those departments to help them bring up their standards and certain people didn't like it, the way I saw it was that they were jealous of our success. It started with silly little things like whispering in corners and up aisles to the canteen falling silent when you walked in. Working in the DIY department wasn't what I had enrolled to do and I didn't like it one bit. I didn't mind helping out in the Garden centre as a good friend called Shaun worked there and we could have a carry on when we were on shift together. Most of the folk in the DIY department on the other hand weren't so great. Most of them would pass the day by sitting in the office with the managers chatting and doing no work or out on unauthorised fag breaks often with the managers. Was it any wonder that their department was failing? I just hated the fact that we had been roped in to do their work while they spent the day skiving and the managers looking on and doing nothing about it.

Cara was a co worker that had worked in both the art department and the diy department and was one of the only ones that I felt I could trust along with my supervisor Julia, Shaun and a few others. She was fun to be around, had asked me as a newbie when I first started working there to get her a tin of tartan paint and I had almost fallen for her joke. When we were all on shift together it was a great laugh but when we weren't I hated work, felt isolated from everyone and felt looked down on. Then our bosses decided they needed us to help more with the tills, the only till I had ever operated was a till when I worked in the newsagents and it was just a bog standard one, nothing like the high tech ones Focus had. I was shy and liked working away in my own little department, hated the fact that I was doing a job that I didn't sign up to do and now with the idea of having to operate the till and have to deal with almost every customer that came in the store I grew to hate my job. They changed the dynamics of the job and I no longer looked forward to my shift.

I started to become anxious of who I could trust. It made me physically ill to a point that I was constantly being signed off work from the doctor and to start with it was a welcoming break. This made it all the worse though as when I would go back I felt like I was being picked on even more so for taking time off. I slowly became depressed and hated everyone and everything. Then the shit hit the fan when I got the results of my smear test. I had been to my doctor for the routine test just two weeks before when I got a phone call followed up with a letter to say I had to be re tested, that this time I had to go through to Ninewells hospital to be checked. It did alarm me a bit to say the least but they gave me no indication of what was wrong. I was tested again and had to await the results. They had found abnormal cells in my womb, pre cancerous cells that if not removed right away would develop into cervical cancer. The C word and that's it, your whole world goes into turmoil, Grandpa had died of cancer, my Aunt had her breasts removed because of cancer and my mum had her lymph nodes removed because of a cancer scare. An appointment was made for me to have laser treatment to burn away the cells and I was told not to worry, that they had got to it early enough for them to take it all away. Mark was away so Mum came with me to the treatment room, waited outside for me. I had to change into a hospital gown with nothing but my bra underneath, they asked me to lay on the bed and attached my legs to stirrups, explained to me exactly what they were away to do and also showed me the camera attached to the instrument they were going to put inside me. Above the doctors head was a monitor where I could see everything they were doing should I wish to look. I was petrified, lay back and clenched my hands, being asked to relax but simply couldn't. They had asked if some students could watch in on the procedure which I said ok, was too terrified to say no being put on the spot them all standing looking at me. I just wanted it over with. As far as intrusions felt this had been the first time I felt so embarrassed. At the time the smear test was the only time I felt undignified but this felt way too much for me to handle. The nurses kept talking to me to keep me distracted while the doctor proceeded to burn away the cells. I looked at the monitor above the doctor's head a few times which was weird, getting to see your insides for the first time. I left that day feeling drained was told that I would be sore for a few days, would have a period with the cramps. After that I had to go for regular smears every 6 months instead of every 2 years.

I was constantly on Marks back about him working away, I craved his attention but when he was home I treated him like crap. I just couldn't function properly. I'll never forget the night I finished a late shift and went straight to the Co-op for a bottle of vodka. I came home slammed the door shut and sank to the floor in the hall and cried uncontrollably, opened the bottle there and then and drank the straight vodka to numb everything out. I felt so alone, so full of pain and hatred that I didn't know how to save myself. I wanted a baby so desperately, had just gone through the procedure at the hospital, was so miserable at work and missed my man so much. I thought about going on anti-depressants but had heard so many bad things about them that I decided not to go down that route.

I don't remember what caused it or what was said but I got so angry one night that I started kicking Mark, kicking him to get him out of our bed, didn't want him near me. Being the man that he is he just walked away, disappeared through to the living room to spend the night on the couch. That wasn't me, I wasn't the violent type. I was always so tired but could never get any sleep, tried Nytol, a sleeping tablet in liquid form but it didn't work. I would sit at the end of the bed in the middle of the night and zone out, stare into the darkness willing my life away. I would contemplate taking the razor to my wrists, would lock myself in the bathroom and sit on the edge of the bath with the razor willing myself to just do it. In the end I just couldn't, I was too weak to even take my own life.

Then a letter arrived in the post to say I had to attend a meeting at work, a disciplinary meeting about my constant absence. That was the final straw, I snapped. I made a phone call to my Mum to see if there was any jobs at the factory where she worked, walked into my work and basically told them to stick their job where the sun don't shine.

Starting my new job was like a huge weight off my shoulders. It wasn't exactly what I saw myself doing for the rest of my life, packing jam jars but really I didn't know what I wanted to do, I just needed out of the job I was in.

Mackays turned out to be not too bad a job. The girls were a great laugh and it felt warming to know my Mum was close by watching over me. There were only a small number of us that worked there so every break time production would stop and we would fill the small canteen. Things were pretty laid back when the boss wasn't about so we had a good carry on.

Over the coming weeks my health started to get better and Mark and I started to think more about planning a wedding than trying to get pregnant. Things between us started to get better and I was much happier, I started to feel like me again. We decided to set a date, September 29th 2004. We had been in the car driving through to Dundee when we started throwing dates at each other, then it hit me. We met on the 29th of September so why not celebrate our wedding anniversary that same day. The date the 29th had already been a lucky day for us being the date we met and then the date we got the keys to our first home. Why not make it a hat trick and use it for our wedding anniversary also.

We started looking at venues. Mark didn't want to get married in Arbroath so we started looking out of town. We looked onto churches but soon realised we would have to go to church prior to the big day and that wasn't us. We eventually settled on a lovely hotel just outside Perth with beautiful gardens and a very traditional Scottish theme inside with its open fire places and tartan carpets.

Exactly a week after booking our venue I suddenly realised that my period was late. It was a Sunday morning and the morning after one of our house parties. I had been off my face on shots and was feeling a little worse for wear. I don't know what made me realise but with everything that was going on I had completely forgot about trying for a baby. Two blues lines on the strip, we were having a baby. New job, wedding booked and now we were going to get what we had been trying for what seemed like a life time to achieve. I was pregnant and we couldn't be happier.

"The children we bring into this world are small replicas of ourselves and our husbands, the pride and joy of grandfathers and grandmothers. We dream of beings mothers, and for most of us that dreams are realised naturally. For this is the miracle of life" _Azelene Williams

Chapter Fourteen

Now that the date was set for the wedding we had to think about who was going to be in the bridal party. Naturally Dillan was to be Marks best man but I didn't really have any close girlfriends to ask. My cousin Danielle was the closest I had so when I asked if she would be my bridesmaid and said yes I was happy. Mark and Dillan came up with the idea to ask Dillan's girlfriend to be my second bridesmaid which I thought was a lovely idea. We had only just recently been introduced but it would be a perfect way to get to know each other.

Kate was a lovely girl, quiet and nothing like I had imagined Dillan to be with. She was very reserved, yet so easy to get along with. A month or so after I found out I was pregnant Kate found out she was expecting also. It was nice to know we were expecting together and that I would have someone to share it with but really between us both being ill and the lack of parties we didn't really share much until after the births.

I must admit that the whole pregnancy thing wasn't what I'd expected it to be. To be honest I hadn't really thought that far. I suppose you could say I was very naive about becoming a mother. I had tried to stop smoking before I fell pregnant but after several failed attempts at it I gave up trying. That was until the morning sickness kicked in. I'd never felt ill like it in my life. I ended up signed off my work for 8 weeks and even after I went back I was still being sick every morning.

During the time I had off I would sit about doing nothing but watch crappy tv to pass the day, got addicted to 'Smallville' and a fly one the wall type programme that had live coverage all day long called 'The Salon'. I had to sprinkle some sort of energy powder on cereal to give me the vitamins and minerals that my body was lacking, I felt terrible 24/7. When I wasn't being sick I still felt sick, had no energy which made me feel depressed. I took it out on Mark, hated him being on the road all the time, by myself all the time. Eventually the sickness subsided enough to allow me to go back to work. By now I was eating like a horse, making up for the fact that one I was carrying a baby and two I was missing my cigarettes. And boy did I pile on the pounds, wearing tacky joggers and strappy tops, hair scraped back in a ponytail. Looking back at pictures god knows what Mark saw in me.

I struggled when back at work. Every morning without fail I would be sick as soon as I woke. At work all morning I would be back and forward to the toilets to either be sick or get a breather. By lunch time I would be feeling a bit better but then the exhaustion would kick in and my whole body would ache. As soon as my maternity was legally allowed to start I was off, couldn't stay a moment longer. The girls at work were great, had a whip round and got me loads of baby presents and vouchers to spend in Mothercare.

I was eight months pregnant, now on maternity leave and getting really big when I was introduced to Marks sister and her children. Scarlet had stopped talking to Mark and their parent's years before Mark and I met but now she was getting divorced and she needed her family to help pick up the pieces. I had heard a lot of bad stuff about her and wasn't too keen about getting to know her but to keep the peace we said nothing.

By now we knew we were having a little girl and had spent months trying to decide on a name. All the girls at work teased me with all sorts of weird and wonderful names but by now we had settled on Shannon Louise Sibbit. She was like a little whirl wind in my stomach always on the go. I remember lying in the bath one night and she started to move about. By this time things were pretty snug in there and there wasn't must room. It was like something out of an alien film, but I loved it. I loved feeling her move about and I loved having somewhere to place my cup of tea while resting in front of the tv. We had decorated the spare room in cream with a Winnie the Pooh border around the top and lovely red curtains to match the new red carpet. With a cot, spare bed and nursery furniture all in place it was all becoming so real. I would shop for baby clothes, wash them and have they all ready for Shannon's arrival, spend sunny afternoons in there relaxing, lying on the spare bed watching the sunlight bounce off the walls, was so peaceful at last when I was alone with my baby girl kicking away inside me.

I was only about 30 weeks when I started to have problems again. I was in and out of hospital with some sort of pain or some infection or another. Mark was still away a lot and often I would have to contact my parents late at night to be taken up to the hospital for checks, be put on monitors. By 33 weeks I was fitted with a physiotherapy belt as I was struggling to carry the extra weight around. I was in a lot of pain and from this I got really grouchy. I missed my man and hated that he wasn't around to look after me properly. I didn't feel like he understood what I was going through and it made me feel alone and even more so of a grouch. He had gone out one night and got blind drunk. Not wanting to have to spend the night next to a drunk while heavily pregnant I decided to sleep in the spare room only to be awoken by him making a racket in the bathroom across the hall from me. He was being violently sick all over the bathroom, standing in front of the toilet being sick all over his clothes as he stood, up the walls and on everything in the bathroom. He stumbled to the bedroom and passed out. I spent the early hours of the morning cleaning up his mess and refused to speak to him when he eventually got up. I can still remember the awful stench of his stomach contents all over the bathroom as I cleaned it up, can smell it as clearly as if it had just happened today. I was the one needing taken care of not him and it frustrated the hell out of me.

It was harvest time and Mark was doing a Saturday shift, he had just left for work at the back of seven in the morning when I rolled over to go back to sleep when I wet myself. I ran to the bathroom then realised it wasn't that I had peed myself, my waters had broken. I was only 35 weeks pregnant. I hadn't even attended any antenatal classes yet. It was too early. I was told to get straight through to Ninewells hospital in Dundee as I had not long found out I had group B strep that was harmful for Shannon when in labour. Mark came straight home and we headed off to Dundee with Mum and Dad close behind. They wouldn't let Mum in so she waited upstairs all day before eventually being told to go home. What a day and night that followed. They had to induce my labour which made it so much more intense than it should have been naturally and they put me on an antibiotic drip for the group b strep. What a site I must have been in front of Mark but at the time I didn't care. My dignity had been left well and truly at the front door as I rushed to the toilet. I had just made it to the labour suite when my bowls opened. Fair to say I was in there for some time as they were almost knocking the door down to make sure I was ok. After hours of intense early labour pains and numerous attempts to pee in a bowl on top of the bed I was given an epidural. I didn't like the sound of it but by now I didn't care, I was in so much pain. From the look on Marks face he didn't like the sight of it. The nurses had to pin me down so that the needle didn't slip as it was inserted into my spine. Once it kicked it and the catheter was put in place I got to relax for a bit until the pains got so intense that I was topping up my epidural constantly and the gas and air was doing nothing for me. I was throwing up left right and centre and in the middle of it all was Mark. He was right there with me through it all, holding my hand, encouraging me and trying to make me laugh. Mopping my brow and holding my hair back while I puked my guts up. I finally had what I had been wanting all this time, my man looking after me. I knew then that he really did care.

At 00.18, baby Shannon was born weighing only 5lbs and 7 oz. It was a very emotional moment and even Mark had tears streaming down his face. She was a blue baby with the cord wrapped around her neck, quickly whisked out the room to be resuscitated in the corridor. She was brought back through afterwards for a few seconds to let us see her before being taken up to intensive care.

A couple of hours after Shannon was born I was wheel chaired up to intensive care to see our baby properly. I was so scared and hadn't felt such exhaustion before. It was dark outside and the corridors were quiet as we got there. We entered through secured doors and along a long corridor that was to become a routine walk for days to come. At the end was a large room filled with loads of incubators with tiny babies wired up with tubes, the room was silent all bar the beeps and sounds of suction as the ventilators went up and down. Shannon was lying on her stomach with a large tube attached to help her breath. We were allowed to put our hands through the holes in the side of her incubator but that was all. After several minutes alone by her side I was wheeled back to the ward to my bed where I had to say goodbye to Mark and almost as soon as the curtain was flung around my bed space I was out. I drifted in and out of sleep for a few hours unsure what was a dream and what wasn't. It was getting light outside already and I had only just gotten to bed. At breakfast time I was awoken by the nurse doing her routine checks to make sure I was ok. I was suddenly very shy again, having a stranger inspect my private parts very closely felt like an intrusion. I needed the toilet and was allowed to go by myself for the first time in 24 hrs. It was strange as my legs although I could feel them were very weak and my hand felt like it still had the drip attached. I was so tired and felt like I was in a dream state. Shortly after breakfast I was moved to a private room so that I didn't have to be on the ward with all the mothers with their babies. It was nice to have my own privacy, my own toilet and a tv to pass the time. Every time I passed urine I had to do so in a bowl so that they could inspect the contents, must be lovely being a nurse having to inspect the after effect of every pregnant woman that passed through their doors.

The days that followed were almost like a dream drifting from one day to another not really knowing what was happening, being scared and not knowing what was going to happen next. I was stuck on the ward while Shannon was still in intensive care and Mark was at home. We finally had our own wee family but were spending our first days apart. Mark came up when he could and I spent as much time as I could learning how to care for Shannon. It was really scary changing that first nappy and trying to feed her. I had wanted to breast feed but at first it wasn't possible due to all the tubes coming out of her tiny body. I had to learn to express my milk and feed it through a tiny tube going in through her nose. That first time I held my baby was such a warm and yet strange feeling. I had never in my life held a baby before and now here I was holding my own tiny baby but in a room with machines constantly beeping and with wires and tubes everywhere. I was terrified to say the least.

I was walking along the corridor on my way to do Shannon's routine changes and feeds when I realised how sore my breasts had become. They had gotten bigger while I was pregnant but now they looked huge and felt like solid bricks stuck to my chest. When I went into the private room to express my milk it was a huge relief, they would become slightly softer but still very tender. They had a mind of their own and would leak everywhere often resulting in me having to change my tops several times a day. Back on the ward even the sound of someone else's baby crying would make them leak. Mark loved it of course and I loved the extra attention he gave me because of it.

When Shannon was 5 days old I got to go home for a night with mark to get organised for Shannon's home coming and also so they had an extra night to free up a bed in Transitional care to be with Shannon properly for the first time. I had nothing at home that would fit Shannon as she was so tiny resulting in us having to use the clothes and nappies that the hospital supplied. The nappies were half the size of the ones that could be bought in shops.

It was strange being home, going down town picking up some bits and pieces for Shannon. I bumped into my old school friend Megan who was also pregnant, due before me but still heavily pregnant. She asked me how I was doing and how long I still had to go. I still had a baby bump so she didn't know Shannon had already arrived. It was the strangest conversation, trying to explain that my baby was already here but I was home for a day to get sorted for her coming home. That night while I was snuggled up with Mark in bed he whispered in my ear that I had made him the happiest man on the earth. It was so sincere and so comforting. I get goose bumps every time I think about it. In that moment although I loved this man dearly and was to marry him I knew this was it. There was no one else and there never would be. I had never felt so much joy.

"There are no short cuts to any place worth going"   _Beverly Sills

Chapter Fifteen

Transitional care wasn't as scary as I thought it might be but it was strange to finally have my baby in a cot by my side. Shannon still had her feeding tubes in and her antibiotic drip but things were on the up and getting home together as a family was soon to be on the cards. I shared a room with another mother but she was only 13 years old. We kept ourselves to ourselves only having the odd pleasantries when we weren't busy with our babies or visiting families. Soon the drip and feeding tubes were removed and I was allowed to attempt breast feeding. I found it all very overwhelming as not only was it hard to get Shannon to feed but I was shy and couldn't do it in front of anyone other than the nurses and Mark. Every time a visitor came I either had to stop feeding her or make them wait outside which was uncomfortable all round. I eventually got the hang of what I was doing and soon Shannon did too meaning that visiting time got less and less as Shannon was always latched on to my breast.

I was still at this point getting inspected on a regular basis from the nurses so it wasn't just Shannon that was being cared for. I felt well looked after and the nurses were very sympathetic to our whole situation. Late one night I had gone to the toilet and had a sudden gush of blood, more so than usual followed but a blood clot the size of a tennis ball. I felt very weak and tired and was monitored very closely for signs of problems. They had taken the blood clot away to dissect it and inspect it further but thank fully there was no more abnormal findings and I was told no more about why it had happened.

After nine days of being in hospital we finally got to take Shannon home. I couldn't wait to get out of there but I was scared. She was so tiny in her car seat with baby clothes on that drowned her. I really didn't know what I was doing. I had to learn as I went and boy was it hard work. Shannon was a hungry baby and I felt like she was never off my boob. I was exhausted and needed help so we decided after three weeks it was time to start her on a bottle so I could get a break. It was a shock to the system that I really wasn't expecting. Mark was still working on the distance lorry driving and I struggled by myself. When he was home he was great with Shannon, always willing to change nappies and do feeds during the day. It was at night that I would curse him. All I wanted was a whole night with unbroken sleep and I wasn't getting it. I grew to learn her cries, when she was wanting fed or changed and when it was for attention. I was shattered and completely drained of the constant screaming so I would do everything I could then give up. I would make sure she was fed and changed then snuggled her in putting her down only for her cries to start again. I would just snap sometimes and would lock myself in another room, would put my ear plugs in and rock myself in a foetus position until I would feel calm enough to re enter the room. I felt awful for doing it but it was the only way I knew how to cope.

Eventually Mum and Dad took Shannon for a whole night for me to try and get a sleep and what happens? Shannon sleeps right through the night, it was a turning point. I was starting to get a better sleep and was now getting into the swing of being a mother. Even though I had lost all my confidence and hated my body Mark and I started to have sex again. We had tried while I was pregnant but I was either always ill or in so much pain that sex was practically non- existent while he was home. Typically the first time we had sex after Shannon's birth the condom split and we ended up at A&E for the morning after pill. To my horror it was my downstairs neighbour who was on duty at the time. As soon as I could I was back on the contraceptive pill to save any further mishaps.

By now Kate had given birth to Flynn and we were able to go out for walks together with the prams, catch up and share stories with one another. The wedding plans were well under way and Kate and I were in fitness mode desperate to lose our baby weight. I would spend most mornings on my cross trainer, GMTV on the tv and Shannon lying down watching me. She would almost every time start to scream only minutes before my 30 minutes were up and I would just let her cry. I tried to stick to a weight watchers diet and started to feel a bit better about myself. I had picked out my dress and was still to get my bridesmaids dresses when the plans took a turn and I ended up with only one bridesmaid.

Danielle was insisting on bringing her new boyfriend who I had known of before she got with him. He was trouble and I just couldn't see what she saw in him nor did the family. Riley was the guy who had lived above Danielle when we had visited with the petrol remote control cars and complained. He was also the guy who got weird on us at the caravan and had been chased away by Danielle's younger brother Mick with a metal pole at one of our parties. She insisted that he stayed with us while she was down for the wedding but I didn't trust him, didn't want him in my house so told her straight. Riley and I ended up cursing down the phone at one another and when she refused to come down for a dress fitting that was it, I told her not to bother. We didn't speak for years after that, still aren't close to this day. It was a shame really as we had been so close growing up and I just didn't understand why she was throwing her life away for some lowlife.

Everything was coming together and the months of planning were almost over. We had our hen and stag do's, nothing fancy just in town with a few friends and we got blackened. My Henny consisted of a couple of friends, my Mum and a couple of her friends, a meal at the local Chinese restaurant then a pub crawl in town. Marks Stag do was a few friends in our local pub round the corner and a stripper in the form of a drunken male friend taking the mick. The blackening backfired on me big time. Marks work mates had secretly arranged to blacken Mark at the works yard one Saturday afternoon while everyone was down there cleaning and servicing the trucks. We were let in on the plan and had all arranged to meet down there for the pictures. Josh, Marks dad had told me to wear old clothes just in case any of us got dirty and the fool I am I fell for it. When we got there not only was Mark mortified of what was happening but soon I was too when they grabbed me and piled me onto the back of the trailer. They piled buckets of who knows what over the top of us both before driving us around town with a convoy of cars containing our family and friends beeping their horns, making everyone turn to our attention. What a laugh it was and having to strip to our underwear in the entry of our flat was hysterical as I struggled to get out of my soaked jeans.

We celebrated Shannon's first birthday just over a month before our big day. All the family was there as well as most of our close friends. We had organised a barbeque at Mum and Dad's back door, Dad had made the birthday cake and between both my parents they made the perfect hosts. I remember feeling slightly over whelmed. Not just at how nice it was to have everyone around us but every time someone mentioned the wedding I had this feeling in the pit of my stomach, like butterflies but it was almost like I was going to be sick. It was so surreal, having a healthy baby daughter and getting married to the man I loved. It was like every little girls dream and I was living it.

Marks sister Scarlet was well and truly under our skin by this point and I actually liked her, couldn't see her for what she really was. I mean she was there to see Shannon after she was born, she was at my Henny and we would go for nights out and visit for coffee. Little did I know of the real Scarlet, boy I was fooled. I suppose the first time I realised something wasn't right was when I had visited for a coffee when she lived on the high street. I had a dentist appointment just down the road from her and she offered to watch Shannon. When I got back all hell broke loose and she had Josh, my soon to be father in Law on the phone. They were arguing and she was making out that they weren't pleased with me for allowing her to watch Shannon and not them. She made them out to be controlling. My second inkling was when she insisted we invite her friend along to the wedding which to be honest I was miffed to say the least. I didn't know her friend and why should I pay for someone when we were on a tight budget as it was. I had wanted my colour theme to be red but when I couldn't find an affordable bridesmaid dress in this colour we opted for the colour of the cheaper dress which was lilac. I had planned everything down to the last detail, had even chosen my flowers and the colours according to superstition and the luck they would bring. Learning that the date we had chosen for our big day was a Wednesday was an even bigger blessing when I learned that it was the luckiest day on the week to get married. It meant that not as much guests would be able to attend with people working during the week but I wasn't willing to budge on the date with its being so sentimental to us both.

I grew nervous a week before the wedding and barely slept or ate a thing. We had a rehearsal in Dundee the day before the wedding and I honestly thought I was going to have an accident in the car on the way through purely because of the nerves. I had planned this wedding almost by myself for over a year now and finally our big day was here. I spent the night at my parent's house sleeping on a blow up bed in the living room. The morning started with breakfast that I couldn't eat followed by a trip to the hairdressers. Mum had to visit the chemist to get me Pepto bismal. I was either going to throw up everywhere or I was going to shit myself with nerves. The hairdresser said she had never encountered someone so nervous before in her life. Once we arrived at The Hunting Tower Hotel outside Perth I began to relax a bit but that didn't last long. While we were getting ready in the honeymoon suite I was pacing the floor waiting for that moment when my Dad would come and get me. Kate and Mum were drinking vodka and coke but I couldn't even look at it. I couldn't believe my moment was almost here and I just couldn't relax enough to just enjoy it. It was almost 1pm now and all we were waiting for was my Dad's arrival.

Then there was a knock at the door and I knew it was time.

"I take you to be my best friend, my faithful partner, and my one true love. I promise to encourage you and inspire you and to love you truly through good times and bad. I will forever be there to laugh with you, to lift you up when you are down and to love you unconditionally through all our adventures in life together."

Chapter Sixteen

By the hotel entrance I stood with my Dad on my arm, red carpet under my feet and a piper awaiting his cue to begin. I had carefully tucked away my wee daughter charm that Dad had given me on his arrival for me. The photographer was taking the last pictures of me before I became a married woman. We walked to the long corridor just before the suite where we were to be married and I tugged ever so tightly to my Dad's arm linking into mine. The piper started playing to warn everyone in the room ahead that we were coming and my heart began to beat hard. This was it, no going back. Mum and Kate walked down first, Mum with Shannon our flower girl in her arms as she wasn't quite walking yet. The piper stopped as we reached the doorway and I looked down the room at everyone staring back at me and went completely numb. I was terrified. Then the piper started playing again and everyone stood to watch me walk down the aisle. I recall seeing the wedding co-ordinator in her wee office just by the side of the door way and giving her a nervous wave and a smile from under my veil and Dad's linked arm. I could see Mark standing there only feet away with tears in his eyes. Perhaps it wasn't just me that feeling so overwhelmed with everything. I turned to face my Dad and smiled as he gave me over to my soon to be husband. Kate took my flowers from my hand and Mark reached over to remove my veil after the minister jokingly asking to remove it to make sure he was marrying the right Mary. Everyone laughed and suddenly it didn't feel as tense as it had been just moments before. We exchanged vows and then the rings. I was so nervous and shaking so much that the minister stepped forward and placed a hand over ours and made a joke about how much my left hand was shaking as Mark placed the ring on my finger. The papers were signed and the piper started up again to send us off out of the room as husband and wife.

"From this day forward, you shall not walk alone. My strength is your protection, my heart will be your shelter and my arms will be your home"
_Dana Marie Bell

Out in the lovely scenic gardens of the hotel we all stood getting our photos taken with the sun beaming down on us. There was lots of chatter and clinking of drinks as everyone stood about socialising. Mark and I looked at one another and I remember thinking wow, we did it.

Afterwards we retreated inside to have of photos taken with the wedding cake that my Dad had made for us. It was to be a surprise, we knew we were getting a cake but didn't know anything about how it would look. It was stunning. With a custom made cake stand in the form of a heart with handmade sugar ivy and thistles entwined around it and three separate tiers with thistles on top. I loved it but suddenly I noticed something was up with my Dad as I looked over from where I was standing, getting my picture taken. Turns out Dad had wanted to see my reaction to the cake when I first saw it and didn't know we had been taken indoors to take some photos, therefore missing my reaction. My heart sunk at that moment. I felt terrible but it had been completely out of my hands at the time.

We were served our meal in between the speeches and I barely touched a thing. With the whole build up of the day and being so ill with nerves I had lost my appetite completely. I was still conscious of eyes on me and I wasn't very comfortable with it. Night came and our evening guests arrived on the bus we had put on. Archie and Maisie from college were with them. Maisie had tears in her eyes and spun me around when they walked in the room. Archie took a stand back to have a proper look at me before coming in for a hug and kiss of congratulations. It made me feel proud hearing Maisie say, "Look at you, you're a married woman all grown up" She was right I had something to be proud of. I had my daughter and now I had a husband.

The first dance was a little awkward as the only dancing Mark and I had done was drunken hip grinding when out on the piss. Lonestar's 'Amazed' was the song we had picked and still to this day when I hear it all I can think about is how much I love my husband. It was hilarious when it came to cutting the cake, every moment caught on camera. The staff came out with a giant cake slicer that's used for cutting wedding cakes and we held it together on the cake and proceeded to cut into the cake while everyone took pictures when Mark decided to make another incision. My Uncle Sam who was recording the whole day on our video camera, the same one we used for that drunken night in our bedroom, said something funny along the lines of "you're not the last Samurai now Mark". I suppose you had to be there but the whole room was in hysterics Mark standing there with a cake slicer that looked like a sword.

There were a few children there on the day so I had made up lots of kiddie parcels and arranged with the DJ to play some games with the kids for prizes. Musical chairs consisted of all the children plus my Mum walking around the chairs with Shannon as she was too small. In the end it was down to Shannon and one other child as the winner. The DJ made them gather as much balloons as possible to determine the winner. Dylan my brother, doting on his wee niece grabbed the most on her behalf and she won. It was so lovely to watch, I loved seeing him with her. It was always like she was turning him into this other being, his face beaming with love for her and I adored it.

In between all the events of the day, Mark and I had retreated to the honeymoon suite to get a breather and to let him see where we were staying for the night. He had of course already seen it when we first got the tour all those months ago but it was a chance for us to get a minute alone. I sat on the edge of the bed hugging him standing in front of me. I just couldn't believe I was finally Mrs Sibbit. I no longer had a different name to not only my husband but also my daughter. We were a complete family now.

My cousin Holly and her friend Lisa had the room next door to ours and on leaving our room we bumped into them and my Uncle Sam. He was long since divorced and now free to play as he wished. He had his eye on Lisa and had been fooling around and flirting with her. I don't think anything actually happened but what's a bit of bonding between guests eh? They were winding us up, wanting to use our jacuzzi bath but we weren't having any of it.

Long after the disco had ended and the bus had left with the evening guests, we stayed up drinking in the hotel bar. I had managed a few vodkas and coke and was feeling fine, a little exhausted but happy. Mark was blootered as we Scots call it, had started the day off with his best man Dillan and a whole bottle of brandy. Holly and Lisa were sitting right across from Mark and pointed out that he was sitting with his legs wide open, a perfect view right up his kilt. I'm sure the pictures are kicking about somewhere that didn't make it into our wedding album. That night I was sure I wouldn't get laid but let's just say that we managed somehow, managed to consummate the marriage.

In the morning we decided not to join our guests in the breakfast room and had breakfast in bed instead. Mark was hung over and I was exhausted. We packed our stuff up and loaded the car only to find it covered with graffiti and roped tin cans tied to the back of it. Just like in the movies we took off into the distance as man and wife, the tins cans trailing behind us and the just married sign on the back window.

"There seems to be an unwritten law that going on honeymoon is like joining the Masons.....secret and mysterious, and fewer questions asked the less embarrassing for everyone" _Martha Byrd Porter

The Yorkshire Dales, I hadn't been before but soon I was going to love it. We had booked a Monday to Friday deal at a lovely wee place called Fawether Grange, a romantic one bedroom log cabin in the middle of nowhere. There were a few other cabins nearby but we had complete privacy. With electronic gates to get in and out, surrounded with trees and lovely countryside it was a safe haven. It was so romantic on arrival, champagne on ice, chocolate laid on our four posted bed, an en-suite bathroom complete with a Jacuzzi bath and a sauna room. Soon we were stripped, bottle of champagne and glasses in one hand and strawberries in another, hot tub time. This of course every time ended up with sex, under the water, groping at each other. Hot tub sex in the rain while it's freezing outside drives your senses wild. I wish I had been less conscious of myself and had been the woman I am today back then. I never appreciated the opportunities that the surroundings had while on honeymoon, let's just say that if I was back there now as the woman I am today I would certainly use every moment to its full potential.

I had worn a lilac bikini into the hot tub, the only time I ever wore one, I had ran into the hot tub so not to be noticed. I still had a little bit of baby weight but had done so well with loosing the excess weight for the wedding. I had a lot of stretch marks but under the right light they didn't look too bad. Looking back at photos I still see myself as overweight but I was happy for the time being, with my body, I had worked so hard. I would never wear a bikini now after having two children. I just wish I had appreciated the body I had back then and had the confidence I have now while love making. It's strange really as back then I had no confidence in the bedroom but wasn't too much fused about my body. Now as I am older I have loads of confidence in the bedroom but am very conscience of my body. Not so much so that it interferes with our sex life but I am on a mission to be better. I have learned how to look after myself and I know what angles and positions of my body look good and which don't, which sexy outfits to wear to cover the bits of my body I don't like, in turn making me feel sexy. I also know now what lighting makes me glow and radiate sex and learning this has made it seem to others that I am confident within my body. I know now that no matter what I was to change about myself there would always be something else that would niggle at me. I have learned to love who I am and live with the body I have been given. This has ultimately changed my life but going back to the time in my life when I was still so naïve to what future lay ahead, I was enjoying our honeymoon and having innocent fun with my husband.

We had an open log fire and most nights we would snuggle up in front of it, drinking and watching tv. I got too drunk one night drinking a bottle of Kola Cube shots and spend hours in the toilet throwing up what looked like blood. The drunken sex before hand was great fun though.

I pined for Shannon while away, she was only 13 months old and we had never left her before for so long. The grannies were taking their turns at spending quality time with her and I wanted to be there too. As much as I loved being the new wife spending quality time with my new husband I felt an ache in the pit of my stomach, I felt guilty leaving her behind.

We spent our break exploring neighbouring towns and villages, visited the television set of the Emmerdale, had bar lunches, went for walks and even fitted in a massage at the local spa. We went to the York Dungeons and boy was I crapping myself. I've always had this fear of werewolfs, had done since I was a child watching 'American werewolf in London'. I had the fear but would still watch the films almost like it was a thrill to be so scared. I'll never go to another Dungeon now though, it was probably the first time I had suffered from heart palpitations and it wasn't a nice experience. Having Jack the ripper jump out at you with a knife will do that to you. There were all sorts of creepy things in there and I'd never felt so claustrophobic in my life. It was a great break in all but I was glad when we got home. It was time to start getting back to normal, time to start looking for a job and time to get used to my new name.

" The greatest gifts you can give your children are the roots of responsibility and the wings of independence" _Denis Waitley

Chapter Seventeen

I had craved my own independence again, wanted to be more than just a mother and now a wife. My maternity leave had ended and because I couldn't go back full time I had no option but to hand in my notice a few months before we got married. We had looked into childcare full time but it was going to cost us almost as much as the wage I would earn so wasn't worth it. I needed something to get me out the house and earning again so started on Job seekers allowance which gave me a small amount of extra money a week but also meant I had to sign on at the job centre once a fortnight.

I had always been in work from the age of 16 and had never asked anyone for financial help before. I hated it, hated been made to feel so small. I would turn up eager to search on their computers and would print out the evidence of my job search from home. We had recently bought our first computer and it was great at aiding me to search all sorts of things I had never looked at before. Every fortnight I would have to sit at a desk being grilled about what I had actually done to try and find a job.

Here I was with a baby in a pram, dressed well, with an obvious record of never being out of work and eager to work again yet every time I was made to feel like one of the junkie low lives that have never worked a day in their life. They belittled me every time and I hated feeling so small. My confidence was low as most mothers can identify with having small children. I don't know what it is exactly that happens after given birth but you tend to lose the person you were before. Your confidence hits the floor and you feel that no one else other than other mums know how you feel. It takes time and the love and understanding of the people around you to bring you back up again. I needed to be in and around adult company again on a regular basis and I needed it before I broke.

After a few months of searching for a suitable position to suit family life I got a phone call from my Mum to say that they were now taking on part time workers at my old job, the business was growing and they were struggling to get full time workers. Brilliant!! I couldn't believe I could get my old job back and only have to suffer a part time shift, my Mum to the rescue again. My hours consisted of Monday – Friday, 9am-2.30pm with a small lunch break in between. Marks parents and my Dad offered to have Shannon to allow me to work so it was perfect.

Although I had worked at Mackays before, I was still very nervous the first few days going back. There were a lot of new faces and a few friendly ones who were still there from before. The job was much the same only this time I was eventually promoted in a sense to also help out with sales in the factory shop and with the internet orders. I loved being off the factory floor and in the shop. I was able to interact more with the public and would be allowed to use my creative flair for doing displays.

Having the extra money was great but it was a lot harder than I thought it would be. Mark being away from home all week, usually only home either on the Friday night or Sat afternoon, then he would be away again on the Sunday afternoon, I hated Sunday afternoon's saying goodbye. Having Marks parents around the corner was a god send. They would have me round for tea, would keep Shannon longer to allow me to get on with housework and having the internet was an extra luxury. I would order my weekly food shop online and have it delivered. I didn't drive and just couldn't afford to taxi it every time I needed a big shop.

When Mark was home or we had the odd weekend together we would make the most of it, family days out with Dillan and Kate and their little boy Flynn, Adult nights out the four of us and romantic diners for two. The adult nights out were fun and on a few occasions resulted in Mark and I having sex in public toilets. It was New Year and we were out in town, Mark had his kilt on and I was learning what it must be like for a man being out with a girl in a skirt. The kilt being made of heavy material meant it was easier to move my hand about underneath without anyone noticing what was going on. We had gotten so pent up that we took it to the disabled toilet and relieved the built up sexual tension between us. On the way home some girl walking up the high street decided to start flirting with Mark and trying to see if he was a true Scotsman. I was livid and for the first time in my life got aggressive over my man. I don't know where it came from but most certainly was because of the alcohol consumption. I didn't want anyone touching my man and certainly not some skank who looked like a prostitute half my age. Luckily the police were walking towards us as it could off ended nasty.

On a night out with Dillan and Kate we had opted to go to Broughty Ferry as Dillan didn't like going out in town. We ended up at some nightclub on the beachfront that I had never been in before. After a lot of dancing and hip grinding on Marks lap we decided to leave and ended up on the beach having sex. It was cold, wet and the sand got in all the places you wouldn't want it to be. It was risky as we could still be seen from the promenade but we didn't care, were fuelled with booze and were frisky, the risk added to the pleasure.

I had started to feel a little unwell, had noticed several changes in my digestive system. I would get cramps after eating and would get indigestion really easy. I had suffered from really bad indigestion and heart burn while I was pregnant and it prevented me from eating a lot of my favourite foods. After a night of partying and taking shots I was woken by a sharp stabbing pain in the centre of my chest and in my back. I took some antacids but they weren't helping. I rubbed on my chest trying to release any wind that I could but nothing would work. I was on my hands and knees on the bedroom floor in a state of panic, Mark using his large hands and firm pressure to rub my back but nothing was working. I ended up on the phone to NHS 24 being told to try drinking warm water. To my relief it slowly started to work and ruled out the possible heart attack that they said it may have been. I was put off drinking shots for a long time afterwards and started to realise that I wasn't young anymore. I had to start drinking sensibly and look after myself more.

When I could I would still go on overnight trips with Mark in the lorry. It didn't happen often having a job and a family but soon it became non-existent. I had been on an overnight stay down to the borders when I suddenly started to feel unwell while Mark was tipping the load before heading back home. I felt nauseous and my stomach started to cramp, setting me into a wee panic as there were no toilets nearby. We had just made it to the nearest village when I threw up in the first toilet I could find. It was a trip home that I will never forget and I'm sure Mark hasn't either. We stopped in almost every village or town that we went through so that I could either be sick or empty my bowels. I had no idea where it was all coming from. In one village I must on been in the toilets for almost 45 minutes and Mark was worried sick , his articulated lorry parked outside on double yellow lines with his hazard lights flashing, holding up traffic in a tiny village. Never again did I go away far in the lorry. It triggered a fear of travelling and lack of toilets that was to last to this day. It got so bad at one point that I ended up having to seek therapy for it.

"Your perspective on life comes from the cage you were held captive in" _Shannon L Alder

I started to have what I now know as panic attacks when Mark was home and in the toilet for too long. I was embarrassed and would never go to the toilet in front of Mark as I saw it as too private a thing to share. I had a problem but was too scared to go to the doctor about it. I learned to deal with it myself by not going on long trips and really Mark wasn't home often so it wasn't very often that I had to deal with his long toilet breaks. I would curse him taking a magazine in there with him but just couldn't tell him how I was feeling, how anxious I would be when he was in there too long. It didn't help that on one occasion I was so anxious about needing the toilet that I just couldn't hold it in. The sweat was pouring off me, my head was in a spin and rather than burst in on him having a shower I stood in the kitchen and had an accident that left me mortified. I had never before in my life not been able to make it to the toilet on time and here I was a grown adult so ashamed of myself. Of course I never told anyone what had happened and to this day I still haven't told Mark what happened that night. I had cleaned myself up quickly, shoved my soiled clothes in the outside bin and jumped in the shower as soon as he had vacated the bathroom. It was the start on an ongoing problem that when least expected would cause me unnecessary stress.

"Life is one big road with lots of signs. So when you are riding through the ruts, don't complicate your mind. Flee from hate, mischief and jealousy. Don't bury your thoughts, put your vision to reality. Wake up and live!" _Bob Marley

Scarlet, Marks sister was starting to show her true colours. I started to feel slightly uneasy around her and when she befriended Marks ex girlfriends I started to get suspicious about her. She would say things to Kate either being stupid thinking she wouldn't tell me or being very clever knowing it would get back to me and play with my mind. She would say things about Marks previous relationships almost as if she was trying to cause arguments between us. When I would pop in for coffee she would suddenly be meeting up with these exes of Marks and

I would have to be in the same room as them feeling inferior. I started to distance myself from her and tried to have little if no contact with her unless I needed to. It was not long after we had got together as a family to organise Marks parents Ruby wedding anniversary party when it all came to blows. Scarlet was still in touch with her and Marks older brother who lived in Inverness and was arranging for a family reunion. I had never met Jacob their elder brother and it soon became clear that Scarlet was playing games with her parent's hearts. They had all falling out with each other many years ago and Scarlet let her parents believe that their eldest child wanted reconciliation and that he was willing to do it for their Anniversary. She had us all believing but it was all a big joke to her, he had no such plans, told everyone last minute that he had changed his mind. When it came to the day of the party Scarlet was meant to be helping but turned up late. I had worked my butt off to make a load of the food and helped decorate. Marks Aunt Penny, Uncle Joel and his cousins and their kids were all there and had mucked in. Scarlet not only turned up late and hadn't helped but spent half the time over visiting some guys who lived across the road, sneaking our booze over to them and allowing her 15 year old daughter to sit and get drunk with these guys. It was the last straw. I didn't want anything to do with her. She could come in and out of her parents lives causing a tornado in her path but she wasn't going to do it with my family. I avoided her calls and wouldn't take much notice of her if she crossed paths in the street or at her mum and dad's. She got the hint eventually confronting me about why I was being off with her.

I was in a clothes shop down the high street with Shannon in her buggy when she spotted me, did a u-turn and approached me inside the shop. She had her daughter Matilda with her and together they started being snarky with me asking why I had been avoiding her. I just blew my top, snapped. I tried to walk away but she only followed me further into the shop. I told her that I thought she was taking the mick out of her family and that they deserved better than that. She wasn't happy and had started walking away when she turned around and told me to ask Mark about his nights away. I was stunned, had no idea what to say.

She continued on to say that he had been picking up his ex girlfriend and taking her away on his trips and that they were having an affair. I was welling up inside and was about to break but instead used every ounce of strength inside me to get angry and scream at her. I'm surprised we weren't thrown out of the shop as we ended up screaming across the shop floor at each other with Matilda having a go at me also. I turned and walked toward the back of the shop, thankfully looking back to see that she had gone. I would either off broken down in front of her making her win or I would have been locked up for assault.

I threw down the cloth items I had picked up and bolted out the shop in the direction on my parent's house. I walked fast with my heart rate going just as fast. Then the tears started to stream down my face. I knew in my heart that Mark would never of cheated on me but I had to ask. I phoned him trying to explain what had happened, hated that I had to do so while he was working but I had always phoned to tell him first when something good or bad happened. He was my best friend as well as my husband, and my first instinct was always to phone him.

He was shocked to say the least and swore that it was all complete bullshit. I didn't need him to say it but it was a comfort to hear. He phoned me back several minutes later to say his sister had phoned him to say I had had a go at her in the town and completely denied what she told me. That was it I told him I didn't want anything to do with her and there was no way she was ever getting to see her niece again. I didn't want Mark to have anything to do with her either as I knew that she would twist and twist until she finally got what she wanted. I couldn't make him but deep down he knew what she was really like. We hadn't wanted anything to do with her when she first came into our lives and now our initial gut feeling was proving to be right.

I arrived at my parent's house to see my Dad and he comforted me with the only way he knew how, hot sweet cups of tea. I slowly began to calm but I just couldn't understand why she would do this to me, to her own brother. Did she really want to break up part of her own family and have the niece she supposedly loved dearly suffer from a broken family? There was something just not right with it all.

In the coming weeks I started to hear things about Scarlet, things that made a light switch going off in my head. She fell out with her friend that had been at our wedding and we spent hours one day talking about all the stuff they had gotten up to, a lot of it having to do with Mark and I. When she had split up with her husband and come running back to her parents she wasn't expecting to find me shacked up with her brother and heavily pregnant. She had grown jealous of our relationship and would plot and scheme behind my back, had invited her friend to the wedding solely because she thought the whole thing was a joke and that she needed her there to stop her from going insane. She would make fun of me all the time behind my back and only made friends with Marks ex's because she knew it would cause friction. She made up the whole affair story by herself and the other girl didn't know anything about it. She wanted her brother to herself and would stop at nothing to get what she wanted. It back fired on her in the end as Mark and I had and always will have a bond that won't be broken. No matter what crap had been thrown at us we seem to work our way through it.

Kiara, Scarlet's not so close friend told me numerous stories of Scarlet's trickery and deceitfulness. Often she would have been roped in as Scarlet's best friend to be part of her plots. She had finally seen the error of her ways when Scarlet turned on her and she couldn't apologise enough for her part in the plans Scarlet made her a part of. Together they had conned old men out of hundreds of pounds, fiddled the system and been very vile people. It made me even more determined not to have anything to do with her.

"Around here, we don't look backwards for very long... We keep moving forward, opening up new doors and doing new things because we are curious...and curiosity keeps leading us down new paths" _Walt Disney

Shannon was a toddler now and we needed a nice secure garden for her to play in. I was never able to hang my washing out as my neighbour was a nightmare and would take away the ropes on my washing days. Shannon was walking now and playing with her toys and Connie downstairs was always complaining about her noise. To be honest her husband's snoring was so loud underneath our bedroom that I'm surprised it was Shannon's noise that bothered her. If we could hear him clearly then they most definitely heard us in the bedroom. God knows how many times we broke that pine bed.

It was time to move on and start looking for another house. I didn't want a flat again as it was a nightmare and I loved the idea of having our own upstairs downstairs. We got the flat valued and then started looking. Luckily we saved ourselves the hassle of advertising when Dillan and Kate approached us wanting to buy it from us in a private deal so that they could finally have their own space. It was great not having the added stress of viewing your house to strangers but the house searching was a nightmare. We fell in love with a house on the opposite end of town, perfectly close to my parents and in the area I grew up in but I didn't drive and it meant I would have to up earlier each morning for work. There were several couples interested in this particular house which made it all the harder. We had to make a decision and quick before we lost our chance. We came in with an offer slightly over the asking price and to our relief they accepted. They were a lovely old couple and had gotten a teddy bear specially made for Shannon and left it on the kitchen counter with a new home card for us for when we moved in, a very thoughtful gesture.

We had our own upstairs downstairs house with front and back gardens, brand new fully fitted kitchen, well decorated and new doors and door facings throughout, It had been well looked after. Not only that but Mark had a large shed fully fitted with electricity to use as a work shop for making the model trucks that he had started doing as a hobby. I had the two bathrooms that I secretly longed for which meant I no longer needed to panic about the bathroom situation and a walk in double shower in the shower room next door to our bedroom that had a fantastic view or the outskirts of Arbroath.

It was great but it was also hard work when Mark was away. I would be up every morning early, have myself and Shannon ready to be out the door at 7.15am We would walk across town to be at Marks parents house for the back of 8. I would have a quick cup of tea with them then head off for starting work at 9am. At 2.30pm my shift would end and I would walk back to collect Shannon, have a quick cuppa and catch up on what she had been doing during the day then walk home and usually be home for around 4pm. Then I would have to see to Shannon, make the tea, bath her and the settle her in for bed. After she was settled I would then get on with the housework crawling into bed at whatever hour I could. On a Thursday and Friday it was a good bit easier as they were the days that my Dad would watch Shannon. I wouldn't have to be up quite so early as my Dad would give me a lift to work and would often collect me leaving me more hours in the day to do what was needing done, allowing me to have a little bit of time to myself once Shannon was settled in bed.

It started to drain on me after several months and I started to get ill again. I was diagnosed with sciatica which I was told was a direct result of the epidural I had when I was in labour with Shannon. The stress I had been under had triggered it and boy did it hurt. I took all the pain killers and carried on not wanting to be the weak mother that couldn't cope. Then my whole body fell under attack. I was diagnosed with carpal tunnel syndrome resulting in me having to wear splints on both wrists and making it very awkward at work but still I didn't give up. Then my old injuries faired up, one being my back injury from when I was a teenager and the torn muscle in my right shoulder from working in Focus. I was in the shower getting ready for work one morning when I started getting pins and needles in my face which then travelled to my entire body. That was it I was officially freaked out and realised that enough was enough. The doctor signed me off work for a few weeks to rest which I did but never did I think that those few weeks would see me never returning to my work again. Big changes were ahead.

"Incredible change happens in your life when you decide to take control of what you do have power over instead of craving control over what you don't." *_Steve Maraboli*

Chapter Eighteen

Mark was finally getting fed up being on the distance with work and decided to look for alternative work. He was missing out on so much with Shannon and soon she would be old enough to attend nursery. I had started going to the gym to get fit and loose what was left of my baby weight, with visiting my doctor regularly due to all the ailments and all that had been happening to me in recent weeks he had suggested it for the feel good factor and for my well being.

Mark had been out to a local company for an interview for a driving position that would mean he would be home all the time and we were on tender hooks waiting for the call to see if our lives were going to change. I had decided to go to the gym while Mark stayed home with Shannon working up a sweat to pass the time, then while walking home I was greeted by Mark and Shannon walking around to meet me. I got a huge hug from an overwhelmed husband with tears in his eyes. He got the job and boy were we both happy. Both our lives were about to change for the better, no more lonely nights and struggling to cope on my own.

" When something bad happens you have three choices. You can either let it define you, let it destroy you, or you can let it strengthen you. "

Mum and Dad had been getting harassed from local teenagers for a while now and they had pushed my Dad to a point of him snapping and taking a hold of one of them. He was being taken to court for assault and was under extreme pressure with everything, when I got a phone call late one night from my Mum in a frantic panic. She was crying and wasn't making much sense but what I could make out was that the doctor had been and had sedated my Dad. (Earlier that night they were getting pestered by the usual teenagers when my Dad had collapsed and had some sort of a seizure) Shannon was tucked up in bed and there was really nothing that I could do so Mum told me to just stay at home as my brother was looking after her. The doctor had checked him over and sedated him to get a good night rest before organising some tests in the morning. Being off my work I took it upon myself to go round and spend some time with him running errands whenever it was needed. After a few weeks he was more settled and decided to go on a trip up north to Inverness for a break when it happened again.

It hadn't even been 24hrs from them leaving when I got a phone call in the middle of the night from Mum to say Dad was in Raigmore Hospital. He had collapsed by the side of their bed and this time they had to get an ambulance. They were running tests and she was really worried. Being up there on her own while Dad lay on a hospital bed out of it with what- ever drugs they were giving him had freaked her out. Mark luckily was home and with my brother we made our way by car to be with her, making accommodation reservations on the way.

Walking into the hospital after a 3 hour car journey with no idea of what to expect was like being in a dream. It felt like time had stood still and that we were never going to get there, all sorts of scenarios in my head on the way up. The last time I had been in this hospital was when I was child. I had been up to visit my Grandpa who was dying of cancer and I never saw him again after that day.

The room was quiet, all but the machines by my Dad's bedside and the sun was beaming off of the ceiling with the blinds tilted up making the room darker and peaceful while Dad rested. Mum was sitting trying to read a magazine and as soon as they heard my voice she leap up to hug me and Dads mouth quirked up at the corner indicating a smile, a smile that was more seen in his eyes than the rest of his face.

He was stable but after numerous tests they had discovered that he had scaring on his brain, he had suffered a series of stokes. He could speak but not as clearly as before and he couldn't move one side of his face properly, it had a sagging effect and they didn't know how long if at all he would recover fully.

After a while Dad was allowed to go home with follow up appointments but wasn't allowed to drive for a while. Mark made arrangements to get us all home safely, driving us all home in my Dad's car leaving his behind, his dad later travelling up to Inverness to pick up his car while Mark was back at work. The weeks that followed I knew that Dad would need extra care. Mum had a full time job and was the only earner in the house and I was off work supposed to be resting when it hit me.

Mark and I had previously been talking about trying to get pregnant again and I had come off my pill to do so, I was off my work and Dad needed someone around. I couldn't rely on Dad to watch Shannon for me to go back to work once my sick line ran out so I decided to hand in my notice. We wanted another child so would eventually have to leave anyway and right now Dad needed me. Within a few weeks of handing in my notice I was pregnant again and everything was falling into place.

"It is the most powerful creation to have life growing inside you, there is no bigger gift" _Beyonce

Shannon was almost at the age where she could go to nursery and had needed it for some time. We would have to pass the local school every day to get to my Dad's or the shops and every time we passed and the children were out playing she would ask to go in and play with them. I got her name down to start and a week before her third birthday she got a place.

Blake was our next door neighbour and during the summer months after moving into our new house we started to get to know him via spending time in the back garden. He had just met his new girlfriend Jasmine via an online dating agency who seemed at first to be really nice. They had their work cut out though as the ex girlfriend was on the war path and late one night after bashing on Blake's front door waking me up, she decided to smash his bedroom window with some of the stones that lay in his front garden. I witnessed the whole thing but decided to stay out of it.

I was jobless again and Dad was doing much better, was almost back to normal. I was free to have lunch dates and days out with Jasmine and we got really friendly. Mark would have nights out with Blake and we would have barbeques in the back garden, sit up late at night in front of their fire pit snuggled up in a blanket watching the sun go down. Those days and nights were great, Shannon out in the back garden with all her new garden toys then at night she would be tucked up in bed while the adults sat out and had drinks. I miss those times and I miss my old house.

When Jasmine found out I wanted another baby she decided she wanted one too. I was a little surprised by this as she had only just moved in with Blake after a short time dating and they were still getting hassle form Blake's ex. When I found out she was pregnant before me I was shocked. We had started trying a few months before I had been signed off my work but with everything that had been going on, the stress of everything, it just wasn't happening.

I'm sure Blake was shocked as he was from our perceptive railroaded into having a baby. According to Jasmine he didn't even know that she had come off the contraceptive pill. I must admit that I was pretty pissed off that she was pregnant and I wasn't, but a few months after she found out, it was my time.

It was early morning and Mark had just got up for work, was in the kitchen downstairs making up his sandwiches for the day when I decided to use the bathroom upstairs to do a test. Within seconds of peeing on that tiny little stick it was confirmed that my suspicions were correct. I ran down stairs into Marks arms in the door way of the kitchen and whispered in his ear that I was pregnant. We both had tears in our eyes as he hugged me tight. He made sure I made an appointment that day to see a doctor and phone him straight away to confirm that the test was indeed correct, which it was .

For a few weeks I felt great, felt like I was on top of the world. This time I was going to be healthy, had started doing our weekly shop filling up the trolley with all sorts of healthy foods. I was munching into an apple, standing on the step of the backdoor breathing in the fresh morning air when I started to feel nauseous just making it to the kitchen sink. Here we go again was all I could think, I should be so lucky!

Shannon was due her two hour induction at the nursery and I was feeling like death. I couldn't sit about feeling sorry for myself this time, I had to try and be as normal as I could. Sitting playing in a room with Shannon with loads of tiny people running about screaming was like Hell for me but for Shannon it was as if she was in heaven. She couldn't wait to go back the next day and luckily for me because she was so eager, I didn't have to stay and play with her. I could go home and feel sorry for myself for a couple of hours. I tried to go on as normal as possible, sitting relaxing when I could to get my energy levels up to run around after Shannon, running to the toilet as often as needed. When I had to leave the house I had to be more aware of where the toilets were just in case I had to dispose of my stomach contents. I can't lie and say it was easier this time around, it wasn't. Only this time I had a distraction in the form of a boisterous 3 year old tom boy daughter and I had my man home at nights to help look after us both.

We had previously booked a holiday to Ripon, not far from where we had gone on our honeymoon. We loved the area when we first visited and wanted to go back and share it this time with Shannon. We booked a lovely little family lodge with its own private hot tub on the banks of a river. I hadn't been pregnant when we booked the holiday and now I was and had to suffer the journey with not only travel sickness but also morning sickness. (I had terrible travel sickness as a child and after having Shannon it had slowly started to come back again) I quizzed my doctor about the whole morning sickness and travel sickness and discovered that being pregnant I wouldn't be able to take my usual travel sickness tablets. I had been given a tablet to dissolve between my gums and top teeth and boy was it disgusting. It was meant to stop me from being sick during my day to day routine but wasn't doing a thing but leave a terrible taste in my mouth. I was then given suppositories, something I hadn't used before and didn't like the sound of. I didn't want anything going near my back side never mind in it but I had no choice, I had to try and get the morning sickness under control before I had to tackle the travel sickness also.

To my relief they worked, well worked well enough to stop me being sick all day. After my initial bout of sickness as soon as I woke every morning and after I empted my bowels I would insert the magic pill and wait for it to work. Once this was in place I was a little more at ease for travelling and because I couldn't use travel sickness tablets I had to wear bands on my wrists that pushed on my pressure points. Even when it was a small car journey to the likes of Dundee I would have to do this. It was something at least, I wasn't being sick as often as before and could at least travel some distance but it didn't take the whole nauseous feeling away completely. I learned to live with it for the several weeks that followed.

We finally arrived in Ripon, our sweet little haven. It had been a long journey for me but I was glad to finally be out of the car and exploring our accommodation for the next week. Our view was beautiful, a balcony overlooking the river with high fences on either side so that our decking and hot tub was secluded. It was then that it suddenly hit me....I couldn't go in our very relaxing looking hot tub, instead had to sit on the sidelines watching Mark enjoy it and Shannon splash about with her water wings on. The joys of what you can and can't do while pregnant, I was missing my Pate too.

Apart from the illness and need for early nights it was a great holiday, we took Shannon to a local theme park and to Hull to The deep. I was quite impressed with The Deep, having a glass elevator that went up right through their giant shark tank. It was great having a child not only for the joy of knowing that they were created by your very existence but also because you suddenly find yourself doing all sorts of different things, having family days out. Mark being brought up to have an interest in transport we visited a transport museum. Shannon got to see Thomas the tank engine, she was very much a Tom boy at that age and loved him and Scooby doo, a theme that was actually used for her 3rd birthday party in our back garden.

"Our children are our greatest blessings"

I was in my second trimester and feeling great, Shannon was loving nursery and making lots of new friends and Mark was enjoying being home with his family. I decided I wanted something to do so I signed up to be an Avon representative distributing books and collecting orders from my family, neighbours and people from neighbouring streets. I loved doing it to start with, getting all these goodies, not actually making any money from it as I would just spend it all on products from the books. It was giving me something to do while Shannon and Mark where out and it was nice to be out and about meeting new people.

I had just found out that Kate was expecting again and it was music to my ears. Not only did we have our first child together but now we were going to have our second. We would meet up when we could, take Shannon and Flynn to the park. It wasn't as easy as it was before now living at the opposite ends of town and neither of us driving but we did what we could when we were both feeling up to it.

Shannon had a new best friend in the form of Blake next doors poodle Robbie. She would be found countless times playing in the back garden with him, I suppose he was her first best friend really. With both Jasmine and I being pregnant we would go out for the day baby shopping. It was her first child and she needed everything. I didn't need much as I still had most of Shannon's stuff but it was still nice to go window shopping. We had decided not to find out the sex of our baby as we wanted a surprise but secretly we both wanted a boy so that we could finally use the name we had wanted to use before we found out we were having Shannon. When it came to the baby scan I just couldn't resist. They had finished my scan and we were leaving the reception when I approached the receptionist to ask if there was any way I could possibly find out the sex of my baby as I hadn't asked. Luckily it wasn't too busy and they took me back in and re scanned me to confirm we were having a wee boy. Poor Mark didn't get a chance to stop me from finding out he just went along with my decision without breathing a word until he found out he was having a son. A dream of most men I suppose having a son, now we were going to be blessed with a son and daughter.

I was 23 weeks gone when I started getting what felt like contractions. I was doubled up in pain and in a state of panic. It was far too early to have my baby. It was another week before they would even attempt to save him had I actually given birth. I was admitted to the maternity ward for close supervision and doped up with different tablets to settle my pains and contractions. It was a very lonely 48 hrs on the ward not knowing if I was about to actually have my baby and if so would they save him. I was really weepy and wanted to be at home but knew that I was in the best place. Thankfully the contractions stopped and I was allowed to go home to rest.

Now that we knew we were having a boy we could make decisions and buy all the boys stuff we couldn't when I was pregnant with Shannon. I had so much pink stuff that I didn't need any more yet I just couldn't bring myself to part with it so it was packaged up and stored in the loft for the time being. We decided we needed a new pram so sold the old one to a young couple who were in desperate need of one then started saving for the new one that Mum and Dad offered to pay half of as a gift. We knew deep down that it would be more than just new prams that would change but refused to think about it for now. We had a two bedroom house that we loved but were soon to have a boy and a girl who would eventually need a room each. I didn't want to move and didn't really want to think about it for now.

Into my 3rd trimester and I was starting to get tired and sore again and wasn't getting much sleep due to the constant heart burn, would find myself falling asleep upright on a stool in the kitchen waiting on my medication to kick in to allow me to lie down. Jasmine had been up and down to the hospital and was now in established labour while we watched Robbie their dog for the night. Ava was a beautiful little girl and newly born when we were first introduced. Holding her was like having a glimpse of what was to come and I felt all warm and fuzzy inside and eager more than ever to meet my little man.

I was 8 months pregnant when we were invited to a wedding up in Aberdeen. We had a room booked in a hotel at the other end of town from the wedding as the hotel itself was way too expensive for us. It was almost Christmas and I was expecting. We didn't need to add to the expense. I didn't really know the couple who were getting married but Mark had become friends with the groom through his work and later I went on to become very close with the Bride. (Skylar would come and visit me on the odd occasion after the wedding and today I class her as one of my closest friends.) We were almost at our digs on the way up when I started to have very strong contractions in the passenger side of the car while Mark was driving. I had to pant my way through them and had images of having to give birth in Aberdeen's hospital. I paced the floor once we arrived at our hotel and was exhausted when they finally stopped. I wished we didn't have to go to the wedding but being pregnant was the perfect excuse to leave early at the end of the long day.

I was starting to get a little worried that I might still have Group B Strep like when I had Shannon but the doctors were refusing to test me for it. There was no current system to test expectant mothers for it and it had been in the media about so many babies dying from it due to one simple test not being offered to women on the NHS. I had been tested the first time when I had been back and forth so many times unwell with Shannon but this time round they wouldn't do a simple swob test to see if I still had it. I was booked into Arbroath as my first port of call for having Jack when doing my birthing plan but I wasn't happy as they didn't have what I needed if I had still been carrying the virus.

With all the recent ups and downs it was taking its toll on my body so I decided to give up my Avon job just as Christmas approached. I thought about carrying it on after the birth but really it wasn't ideal with a new born baby. I did my last campaign which was the Christmas one and said my goodbyes to the customers I had met over the previous months.

It was Christmas morning and I still had 4 weeks left of my pregnancy when I almost fell down our stairs. I was mid way down when I started getting contractions again, grabbing the banisters to stop myself falling. Shannon had opened her presents and was having a ball with her new ride in electric car sat in the middle of our living-room floor. I was feeling exhausted and really wanted to just rest so that's exactly what I did until it was time for dinner. The contractions yet again subsided allowing me to continue with Shannon's last Christmas before she would have to share it with her younger brother.

Two weeks later I started to feel a little funny. It was almost 1am in the morning of the 8th of January when I woke up feeling disorientated and sweating. I rolled over to sit up at the side of the bed when I felt a little trickle down my leg. I managed to walk to the toilet down stairs as I didn't want to wake Mark by just going next door. He had work in the morning his first day back after his two week Christmas holiday and I didn't want to disrupt his sleep. I had just sat down on the toilet when I felt a gush between my legs, my waters had broken. Holding the cold sink as I sat, I settled my forehead on it and felt my head spin. This was it, it was happening again.

"Motherhood is a place where all love begins and ends. It is a journey not a destination. A mother understands what her children do not need to say, a mothers love precieves no impossibilities. Motherhood is a blessing."

Chapter Nineteen

I grabbed myself a sanitary towel and rushed upstairs to let Mark know that my waters had broken. I think he thought I was joking and just rolled over in a daze to fall asleep again. I phoned the midwife, she asked me some questions and then proceeded to say that she had booked me in for 9am to get checked over and see how I was progressing. I was stunned, that was still eight hours away. Fair enough I wasn't in a lot of pain but surely they weren't going to leave it at that?

Then I had a sudden urge to go to the toilet and empty my bowels just like the last time. I must off been sitting there for about half an hour before I finally felt comfortable enough to stand and exit the bathroom. Then the pains started almost 45 minutes after my waters initially broke. To start with they weren't too bad, were like having period cramps. They started to get a little worse and I decided to phone the midwife back. Once she realised it was my second baby she asked me to come in to be checked just in case I was progressing quickly. I woke Mark and asked him to take Shannon over to his mums before coming back for me. He thought we had ages to go yet as it seemed like forever with Shannon's labour. He was gone for almost an hour, had sat and had a cup of tea with his mum before heading back to collect me. By the time he got back I was on my knees on the living room floor panting out my contraction in a panic because he wasn't answering his phone and I was all alone. He took one look at me and went white, then going into overdrive, realising I was indeed in labour this time, no more false alarms.

It was now after 3 in the morning and we had finally arrived at Arbroath hospital. They inspected my cervix in between contractions and confirmed I was already 5 centimetres dilated. I was far enough gone to be allowed into the birthing pool. They started to fill it and Mark and a midwife helped me undress my bottom half and climb in when it was only half filled, just enough to cover my bottom half. It was nice at first but I was very conscious at this point of being naked from the waist down in front of everyone. As the contractions got stronger I was allowed gas and air and to start with it was making me feel nauseous. As I progressed I believe everyone around me thought I still had a while to go as the midwife kept leaving Mark and I to ourselves only occasionally coming back to check my vitals. My back was in agony and I was very uncomfortable being in the sitting position, they still hadn't filled the birthing pool right up as they said there was plenty of time. Eventually the pain had gotten so bad that the midwife offered to give me an injection but I would have to come out of the birthing pool. I was offered an ambulance up through to Ninewells hospital to get another epidural but I would have to wait for it but for the meantime they wanted me out so that they could check me properly. They were worried that Jack was back to back causing extra problems and that's why I was in so much pain already. I remember Mark and the midwife having to lift me out and take off the rest of my clothes so that they could dry my body but they ended up having to hold me up as another really intense contraction hit. Standing stark naked being held up by two people is a thought that makes me cringe and think what a terrible sight it must off been. I at the time was off my head between the pains being so close together and the effect of the gas and air to care. They got me on the bed and the midwife proceeded to check my cervix before administering the injection that in the end I never got. There was no injection, no ambulance just a big grin from the midwife as she took one look at me and said I could push. I had had an overwhelming need to push while I was in the birthing pool but almost like when your bursting for the toilet and don't want an accident I held it in because I didn't want to make a mess. I realise now that this is what the feeling was, it was my body telling me to push. I hadn't had that feeling with Shannon as my bottom half was numb with the epidural. Mark held my had and I squeezed it like mad barely making a sound as I bore down and excepted what was happening to me. I wasn't pushing for long when I finally delivered the head was told to feel between my legs. It was so alien like, like having a huge growth stuck between my legs and the burning sensation that occurred right before the head had popped out was crazy. I had heard about the burning sensation and how you have to pant your way through it but this was amazing. Mark was able to watch as I made my final push and Jack flew out of me being caught by the midwife at the end of the bed. I was so over come with joy and Mark clearly was too as he cried like a baby seeing his son be born, he held my hand and kissed my forehead almost like a powerful acknowledgment of the achievement of the events that had just unfolded before him.

It was five minutes to six on the Monday morning and I had a healthy baby boy weighing 6lb 10oz, the same day and same time as his dad strangely enough. I was allowed to hold my baby as soon as he was born unlike with Shannon and boy was it emotional. He was at first sight a spitting image of my brother. Shortly afterwards while I lay in the bad watching Mark giving Jack his very first feed, in awe of the site before me, Mum and Dad arrived to meet their grandson. Mum was meant to be my second birthing partner but when I had called a few hours earlier she had chickened out of seeing her daughter in pain and left me in the capable hands of my husband. She was up and on her way to work and had popped in before her shift started.

After our short visit I was allowed to have a shower and was feeling rather weak and extremely tired after the night events but I went anyway to freshen up. I had been left alone to shower and it wasn't until I looked down to see the mass of blood in the shower basin below me and running down my leg that I started to feel faint. I sat on the base of the shower as the water cascaded over me until I came too well enough to stand and dress myself in a fresh pair of pyjamas, wearing two hideous maternity sanitary towels to soak up the mass of blood. I was given a room to rest and Jack lay by my side in his cot while Mark was sent home to rest also.

That afternoon I was awoken by a very worried looking husband. Jack wasn't by my side and he had thought something had happened. The midwife's had taken him away for a few hours to allow me a good rest. It's all so surreal thinking back now but at the same time it feels like it was only yesterday. I had decided that I wasn't going to breast-feed Jack after what happened with Shannon's feeding routine , this time Mark was going to be hands on to help me from the word go.

It's strange thinking back about all the little things, all the stuff that they don't actually explain to you about having a baby. The after pains from giving birth the second time round were far more extreme than the first time, I was constantly asking for more pain killers, watching the clock to see when the next round was coming. The stinging sensation when I went to pee and I was lucky having only a graze in my never regions, god knows how it would feel if I had properly tore like some women do? Then there was being scared to empty my bowels as I felt like my whole insides were going to fall out and the dreaded pelvic floor exercises. I was told to do them and given a leaflet on what I had to do but really there was no way of knowing I was doing it properly unless I couldn't stop peeing myself when I laughed, coughed or even sneezed, that's the worst. There's also the fear which a lot of women face but don't talk openly about almost like a taboo. Will their vagina opening ever go back to the way it was before? Will I be too slack to enjoy sex again? Will he see me as too loose and therefore not like sex with me anymore? Crazy thing to be thinking about after giving birth but after the initial few weeks of motherhood, these are the things that I was thinking and I know that others thought too. It was silly really to be thinking this as I knew Mark wasn't shallow enough to think any less of me, after all I had given him two beautiful children. I did wonder though, wanted to still be able to enjoy sex. Yet again I had gone through almost the full pregnancy without sex and this time Mark hadn't pestered me one bit for it. We did try a few times but I had no libido what so ever so it was pointless.

Shannon was really jealous when Jack was first born. We knew she would be as she had been spoilt by everyone and now she had to share all the attention. I had bought her a nice present in the form of a book called 'I'm a big sister'. At night in the hospital Shannon came up to visit us and meet her little brother. At first she wouldn't come near us until I took her to the day room, just the two of us leaving Mark with Jack and sat and played with her with the toys they had available. Slowly she became more like herself then I took her back to see her daddy and little brother. We got her to sit with him and we all sat as a complete family for the first time. Shannon helped her dad feed Jack and watched as I changed his nappy. We gave her the present from Jack and sat and read the story to her. She loved books so it was a perfect gift.

We were only in the hospital a couple of days when we were allowed home. It was so much easier this time round, even having another child at home. It all came flooding back and came natural this time. Having Mark home at nights was a god send. He would help with everything apart from the night feeds which was fair enough as he had a job to go to each day. I did get a little ratty with him on the odd occasion though but only because I was tired and sometimes even if it was the weekend I would wish for him to wake up and take over. Mark could be a nightmare when it came to sleep. When he was asleep that's it there was no waking him. He once slept through the smoke alarm going off outside our bedroom but thankfully it was just dust and not an actual fire. If he drinks too much he just falls asleep and I've had to leave him in some weird positions. I would be surprised if he even heard Shannon and Jack cry through the night when they were babies.

I would sit up in the living room in the middle of the night to feed Jack almost falling asleep watching the first season of 'Skins' on E4. It became almost routine and I would be sat down at the same time in the early hours catching up with my tv programmes as I fed and settled Jack. Jack was a very sickly baby. His birth had been so fast that some of the mucus from within my body had got caught in his tubes. I was told it wouldn't be a problem and that it would clear itself but meantime we just had to deal with him being sick after most feeds. He also had an infection in his eye but again it would be ok. I had to clean it with cooled boiled water each morning, night and whenever it was weepy during the day. He was no longer looking like my brother but has throughout the years definitely developed some of my brother's characteristics. From having the eye infection he is prone to conjunctivitis like my brother, has a temper like my brother and can be a fussy eater like my brother.

I had developed a growth on my index finger of my left hand. It started off looking like a tiny red dot which soon got bigger and started to grow outwards like a giant blood spot. It was painful so I had to seek medical attention only to find out it was some sort of popped blood vessel from squeezing Marks hand during labour. It had something to do with my hormone levels meaning that it hadn't healed itself properly like it should of meaning that I would have to have it operated on.

I was petrified at the clinic that day. I went alone as I had no idea how long I would be there. I had to lie on the bed and they numbed my hand via a needle. I was shaking like a leaf and feeling nauseous but the porter kept talking to me about my life to keep me distracted while they sliced and pulled and prodded at my finger before stitching me up. Although I could feel all the tugging I didn't feel any pain. I had never had stitches before and I couldn't help but wonder how sore it would be to get them taken out. About a week later I had to visit the nurse to get them removed and boy was I scared. Silly really thinking how little a thing it was, I had given birth twice but right at that precise moment they seemed like a breeze compared to this. I had always had a weak stomach and fainting at the slightest thing wasn't uncommon, fainting when I got my belly button pierced, again when I got my tattoo and also when I had jammed my finger in the sliding door when I was little. I knew the signs for it going to happen and I could feel it building up inside me. The nurse must off noticed it too as she helped me to lie down on the bed and continued to talk to me to distract me from what she was doing. It was over in a flash and all the panic had been for nothing. It had all been in my head and I had worked myself up over nothing. I still have a wee scar there today and on cold days it throbs, my own little war wound from giving birth to my baby boy.

Everything was getting back to normal and I was enjoying having not only Jasmine to share my happy baby moments with but now Kate had given birth to a little girl called Felicity. Shannon was continuing to enjoy nursery and was going to start her second year there before finally starting school. Mark loved his new job and our sex life was getting back on track now that Jack was in his cot in Shannon's bedroom next door. We had continued having our little parties in the back door with Blake and Jasmine when we were pregnant minus the booze but now we could crack open the bottles of wine and eat bucket loads of pate, life was great.

Blake was into remote control helicopters and we would fly them on the large grass area in front of our houses. I had been given a shot and to this day we have no idea where it landed. I accidently flew it right over the roofs of our houses and it just vanished, it was so funny at the time and luckily Blake thought so too, he has never let me forget it though. Never leave me in charge or a remote unless it's for the television.

"Sex is....perfectly natural. It's something that is pleasurable. It's enjoyable and enhances a relationship. So don't we learn as much as we can about it and become comfortable with ourselves as sexual human beings as we are all sexual?" _Sue Johanson

It was a lovely summer day and we had invited Dillan, Kate and the kids over for drinks and a barbeque. It was now dark and the kids were tucked up inside sleeping while we carried on drinking. I had recently bought some fairy lights for my parasol and it was still quite warm so it was nice out. Dillan had brought over some pot for us to try and I was a little giddy about it, I hadn't had any for so long and was eager to try it again. I had been stopped smoking for almost 4 years but was willing to have a few puffs just to get its affects. It had a sort of calming effect on me and shortly afterward we all decided to go to bed. Dillan and Kate decided to stay the night so bunked in together on some fold out beds in the living room downstairs. When we got to bed Mark just couldn't keep his hands off me. Smoking pot always seemed to have this effect on him that made him hungry for me, hungry for his head to go between my legs and I loved it. I loved how spontaneous he was in the bedroom. He was always willing to try new things. He had never given up on the idea of having anal sex and that night well let's just say he made a good effort at getting my body ready for it. I had never felt such a sensation in that part of my body before. It felt naughty, it felt dirty but boy did I like it. We didn't have anal sex that night but his hands and his mouth did a whole lot more that they had ever done to me before. It was a small glimpse of what possibilities lay ahead.

"We travel not to escape life, but for life not to escape us."

We had a massive bond-fire night celebration that year getting some of the neighbours and our friends up for a night of drinks and fireworks. Blake had spent a fortune on the fireworks and together we chipped in with food and drink for everyone. It was a cold but dry night and Mark and Blake were in charge of the firework display that they set off from the large grass area out front. We were so lucky that night that no one was carted off in an ambulance. Blake set off one particular firework that took off in the direction of our two gardens. Most of us were indoors watching from the patio doors but Mark and my brother were standing just outside Blake's garden when it flew towards them, they took a dive over the hedge missing its collision. They looked like they had seen a ghost when it happened but everyone was in hysterics at their antics. Jasmine and I stepped in and made sure there were no more drunken fireworks getting set off and the night just turned into a big street party.

We decided to buy a touring caravan after much persuasion from Mark. I wasn't keen on the idea at first when he came home with the idea having been speaking to someone through his work. He took me around some dealerships to let me see what it was all about and he got me hooked on the idea. We managed to get a loan from the bank through our mortgage and bought our first wee 5 berth caravan complete with living area, toilet, kitchen and eating area that converted into bunk beds for the kids. We had traded in the Mega for an Astra when Shannon was born and then bought a Mazda 6 with the money we made from the sale of the flat so it was more than capable of towing the caravan. We took the caravan to Forfar as we had heard it was a nice spot and it wasn't far for doing a test run. It was great being away for only one night coming home feeling refreshed and it was cheap as chips as most sites charged pennies for the use of their site, It became our means of escape.

"Life is the most difficult exam. Many people fail because they try to copy others. Not realising that everyone has a different question paper."

Jack was now teething and the calm nights that we had grown used too started to become disrupted again. It was Shannon that I felt sorry for as she had to sleep in the same room as her younger brother and had to go to nursery every morning. It was time to have the discussion of moving. I really didn't want to move as I loved our little house and the whole set up but I knew our children needed their own space. We got a local company to come over and price the house eventually putting it on the market. I hated having to constantly have my house spotless for viewers as it was hard having a baby and 4 year old in the house. We looked at some properties to buy but our hands were tied until we found a buyer for our house. A few good ones were lost all because we couldn't sell our house fast enough. Then Blake and Jasmine decided they were moving too. I was a bit pissed off because it seemed that everything we wanted to do they wanted to do better. They had just put in a brand new kitchen, had decking, patio doors and we had none of that. It was like going into competition with each other. I knew it was all Jasmine's doing, her family had money and she enjoyed the finer things in life. She was always complaining that the house wasn't big enough for the three of them. When I had told her about suffering from IBS she had to go one better and had Crones disease. I later found out that she never had the disease but in fact made it all up to get us to feel sorry for her.

I had started getting pains in my stomach and having problems with my bowels like I was having before I was pregnant. I decided this time to go to the doctors as I hadn't before as I was too ashamed to admit I had problems in that region. I was soon diagnosed with IBS and given tablets to help keep it under control. They helped the pain but the physiological damage had already been put in place and continued to disrupt my life when I least expected it. I had to take tablets 3 times a day before meals and was given other tablets to control the flow of my bowels that I had to take as and when I needed. It was the relief that I needed and the bloating started to disappear. It was so embarrassing to a point that I was standing in my kitchen one day and my stomach was obviously bloated because of my IBS that Marks mums actually came out and asked me if I was pregnant. I so wanted to slap her right there and then, such a horrible way to find out from someone else that you look fat. I was fine everywhere else but I could see her point as I did have a neat rounded belly on bad days. I was mortified and it made me feel so small and ugly. I had found out my problem so now it was time to get on top of it and show the world that I wasn't fat, well not excessively fat. I was of average size, a size 14 still but it didn't bother me until that horrid moment in my kitchen. I had suddenly become more aware of how I looked to everyone else.

"I find the great thing in the world is not so much where we stand, as in what direction we are moving. To reach the port of heaven, we must sail sometimes with the wind and sometimes against it – but we must sail, and not drift, nor lie at anchor." _*Oliver Wendell Holmes*

Eventually we found a buyer for our house and started looking again for property to move into. I was starting to think we would have to move into our caravan when we got a phone call to say that a house we had previously wanted was back on the market as the sale had fallen through. We went back to view it and fell in love with it. It had a huge back garden with loads of potential, a double driveway perfect for the caravan and the car right at our door meaning no more storage fees for the caravan. It had three bedrooms, one quite small but still perfect and attic way larger than what we had and it had the fireplace that I had always wanted, perfect for hanging a garland on at Christmas. Its downsides on the other hand were that I would no longer have the pretty spindle banister staircase and there was a lack of second toilet and no walk in shower. I hadn't had a toilet panic attack for a long time so I thought it would be ok.

Every house we had viewed I had viewed with an image in my head of what it would be like for having a party. Jack was away to be celebrating his first birthday and we were going to hold a winter wonderland party for him. I knew what I wanted as I had planned all Shannon's previous parties and had a talent for it. When viewing I would think to myself what each area could be utilised for when having parties and this house was perfect, a huge living room decent sized kitchen and each had a door leading off from each other meaning that you could actually walk right round the ground floor in one big circle. We could party downstairs while the kids slept upstairs but the only downside would be that people would now have to go upstairs to the bathroom next to where we all slept but it was a small price to pay for the right house.

We put our offer in only to be told it was refused, the seller had decided to put the house to a closing date as there was a lot of interest in it. We made an offer of £ 113'290 using our current house number, number 13 and our lucky numbers 3 and 29. It was hell waiting to hear if the house was ours or not, then I got the call from the solicitor to tell us to get the champagne out, we had won the private auction.

"I give you this to take with you: Nothing remains as it was. If you know this, you can begin again, with pure joy in the uprooting" – *Judith Minty*

Chapter Twenty

It hadn't taken too long to pack up our nice little home. I had already started boxing up stuff that wasn't used before the sale of the house went through. We had essentially taken the first offer that was made on our house which may off been fairly stupid but it was running up to Christmas and we wanted to spend it in our new home and not in a home that was already covered in boxes. £100'000 we got for our lovely wee home so almost £30'000 was in our pockets to do as we wished. We decided to spend it wisely, put down the deposit on the new home and pay off our loan.

It was the 9th November, moving day and boy was it crazy. The couple moving into our home were given the keys too early by their solicitor and we were still moving the ground floor contents into the van on our second run when they turned up. We had emptied the whole of the second floor so allowed them to move some of their stuff upstairs while we continued to load up the van with what was left. Legally we didn't have to do it as the solicitor had fucked up but they seemed rather disappointed to see us still there when they arrived. It was to be their first place together and as a young couple they were eager to get into their own space.

I remember walking about in the now empty living room, footsteps echoing on the wooden floors, looking out the living room window across the grass where we had had many a kick about with Shannon's football and I felt a little glum. I could hear the new owners upstairs in Shannon and Jacks old bedroom laughing and smiled to myself. I was giving up the home that I loved but someone new was going to enjoy it as much as we had. It was an end to an era and it was going to be strange living in a street where we knew no one, I was going to miss having the neighbours that we had grown so close to.

Our new neighbours were lovely. A little old couple who

doted on Shannon and Jack on one side of us and a family on the other who had a daughter that ended up being one of Shannon's good friends, until they eventually moved on.

It took us weeks to unpack all the boxes properly and had had to order new bedroom furniture for our room as we had built in wardrobes at the old house. The new furniture was coming from MFI and unfortunately it was going to be after Christmas before it would be delivered. Mean while Mark and I had to live out of suitcases and black bin liners.

Christmas came and went and soon it would be Jacks 1st birthday. The winter wonderland theme had all come together and I had loved planning it all. Between that, Christmas and the unpacking it had been a very busy couple of months and this was our chance to really enjoy ourselves. I had purchased wall scene setters for the living room that made the walls look like we were in the middle of a winter snow shower with icicles hanging from the ceiling. I had an igloo tent that was filled with baby blue and white balloons for the kids to play in and a blue cascading drinks fountain. There was a firework display in the back garden, Dad made a snowman themed cake and we had a champagne toast to my perfect, handsome, little man who was now almost walking, standing on his feet but not quite taking the steps yet.

Shortly after Jacks birthday he began to walk. He was proud of himself, a cheesy grin on his face as he pulled himself onto his feet in the kitchen and suddenly started taking steps towards me. Shannon was still in her second year at nursery and was ready for school after the summer. It was time to put her name down and I had to put in a letter of request for her to stay at the school where she was going to nursery. Now that we had moved we were out of catchment area but I didn't want to move her. I didn't want to unsettle her and I was in no way going to do to her what happened to me as a child. It was only really an extra 5 minutes walk to keep her at the school and thankfully they accepted my request.

Blake and Jasmine had got their house sold shortly after we did and had bought this beautiful house just out of town. We kept in touch, started doing dinner parties which made it all the more worthwhile travelling to see each other. I loved to cook and this was a great opportunity to show off what I could do, 3 sometimes 4 course meals were a breeze if I was enjoying it. I would try to do a good spread at Christmas time but this was a chance to do it with so much more than a chicken dinner. I would pick out specific wines to go with whatever I was cooking and felt like I was in my element in the kitchen. Sometimes it would be proper hearty meals like roasts, stews etc and sometimes it was fancier with things like Salmon, stuffed chicken, soufflés etc. Jasmine and I would be in the kitchen helping each other out drinking wine while Mark and Blake would be kicking about doing men stuff, drinking beer and watching the kids.

Dillan and Kate would still come over for nights of drinking and catching up but now that I had discovered the art of the dinner party we would have them over for meals but it would be more casual with things like Mexican dishes and homemade curry nights. We had always been able to talk openly to them about sex and Dillan loved to wind Kate up in front of us. It would always cause some sort of argument between them but despite the arguments I enjoyed their company.

From what we could see Blake and Jasmine were happy and Jasmine loved to on every opportunity available rub it in my face. I must admit I was a little jealous, not of their relationship as I couldn't off been happier with mine with Mark, but of the house they had and the money to go with it. Jasmine's parents had a lot of money and had helped them to purchase their new home and boy was I in love with it. It was a new built house in a quiet little culdy-sac, double drive, huge reception room with high ceiling and lovely open stair case, a downstairs bathroom, a small bedroom, large living room with patio doors, huge kitchen/dining area with patio doors and a door that led to an utility room that also led to a huge double garage with electric doors. Upstairs they had two double bedrooms and family bathroom and another double bedroom the same size as the two other upstairs bedrooms put together with a large en-suite with a double walk in shower. I was in awe of their new home and wished one day to be able to afford something like it. Jasmine would always go on about how great it was not living attached to someone else, how spacious their house was and on and on. I started to feel really inferior at her constant digs that we had a smaller home and were living a fairly normal life compared to her high life. They had both bought new cars and she would go on about how great they were and how fantastic her life was little did I know it was all a facade.

Blake was always very open about the fact that he loved his old home and that if it hadn't been for Jasmine's persuasion he wouldn't off moved house. We distanced ourselves from them for a while as my live was moving on in other directions and they were apparently still living the high life. Blake worked away a lot so when it came to birthday parties, most of the time Jasmine would come alone with the kids. She had fallen pregnant again and had a little boy called Aidan. Eventually she stopped calling, stopped replying to my messages. Blake though, although we don't see much of him he still remains a friend even after their relationship broke down. I still miss our long summer nights in the back garden having drinks and sitting by the fire pit, the great banter and laughter. Remembering those nights always puts a smile on my face.

"I believe that without memories there is no life, and that our memories should be of happy times" _*Lee Radziwill*

"Each friend represents a world in us, a world possibly not born until they arrive, and it is only by this meeting that a new world is born" _ Anais Nin

Chapter Twenty One

Shannon had grown to be a very popular little lady at nursery making loads of new friends and now I was too. Bumping into the mums at the school gates and having a yap was a daily occurrence and we started to socialize away from the gates. We would go for breakfast after dropping off the girls and have girly nights out. No two of us were the same so it was nice to all have our different personalities to bounce off of one another.

Skylar who I had now known for a while, who's wedding I had been to while pregnant with Jack, had a girl Chloe who was at nursery with Shannon, was a year younger but they both attended the morning session together. Skylar liked nice things a bit like Jasmine but in a way that was less in your face. She was very much straight to the point and could be seen as a little bit in your face to anyone who didn't know her properly. Skylar was a good ten years older than me but a lovely caring person to have as a friend. She had been a registered childminder when we first met and became very helpful to me when I decided to take it up myself.

Nancy I had known of from years ago while I was at school but we didn't actually know each other. We would pass each other on the way to nursery most days when I lived in the old house and never spoke a word to each other. I was slightly intimidated by her as she looked stunning and like someone I wouldn't want to cross, turns out that she was intimidated by me at the time also, funny that really. She was the baby of our group of friends being 4 years younger than myself. Nancy had a daughter called Katie who was at nursery with Shannon and a son called Kian a year older than Jack. Nancy was very private like myself and had been a single mother for a lot of her kid's lives, had a boyfriend called Mackenzie, but was very independent. She gave off the illusion that she was a strong woman with loads of confidence but really when you got to know her she didn't have the strong persona that she led everyone to believe. She was at college studying to be a hairdresser relying on her childminder to watch the children when she was busy. She was very much different from me in the way that she didn't have the close nit family unit that I had grown up with.

Tess had a daughter called Annabelle also in Shannon's class at nursery and a son Kai who was ages with Jack. Tess and I had met years ago but I didn't actually know her. I had gone to school with her brother who had been in Danielle and I's group when we were teenagers. Tess was a couple of years older than me, a very outgoing bubbly character, a single parent and cousins with Nancy.

Nadine was ten years older than me, married like myself and Skylar but the tom boy of the group. She had Lexi who was ages with Shannon and also in her class and Cerys who was ages with Jack. Nadine was very in your face, was often on the war path if she wasn't happy with something or someone. She liked her gossip and for a long time I didn't know if I could trust her or not. She never wore make up like myself at the time and loved football. She worked in a local pub and with her husband they would attend all the local and international football matches. Nadine was also a cousin of Tess's but from the other side of the family to Nancy.

Then there was Keira who was a single parent to two daughters, the youngest being Amber who was in Shannon's class, a very independent and private person who worked part time, a few years older than me. Catherine was another mum who would sometimes socialise with us but not very often. She at the time only had Cole who was in Shannon's class. Lois was a friend of Nancy's who lived in the same block of flats as her and she would come out with us on girlie nights out. She was younger than me and very loud and so sure of herself, had a daughter called Mari who was ages with Nancy's Kian. And last there was Kacy who had a son called Ronnie who was also in Shannon's class, also had a daughter who was ages with Kian and Mari. She was married and worked part time at the doctor's surgery. She was the chav of the group, would wear make- up but liked her track suits.

I was very tom boyish myself until I met these girls, was shy around people and was usually seen in jeans, Catapillar boots and strappy tops. The more comfortable I became around my new group of friends the more their personalities rubbed off on me. Having nights out, I would start putting on makeup, learned how to put on fake eye lashes and doing something other than scrape my hair back. With Nancy and Tess around who loved their hair and makeup, I was soon transformed into another person. I started to buy more stylish clothes for our nights out and I suddenly had several shopping companions like having my own style guru's. I started wearing heels, would buy nice matching underwear to go under my short dresses and I felt sexy. I had never felt sexy before and Mark loved the change in me. I started to change in a way that I never thought possible. I actually had confidence again. When I looked good I felt good. When I was feeling down I would dress up and with that, made me feel better about myself. I had girly friends that I could talk openly about all sorts of things including sex and nothing was taboo. There was no holding back on the topics of conversation between us and often we would liven up quiet cafes with our banter. I had never had this before and now I understood what it was like to have a proper group of girlfriends.

I joined the Parent Council at the school and attended all of their meetings, helped organised fund raisers, proms and voiced my opinion on how the school was run. I was growing more and more in confidence now with my new found family and felt like I had a voice. I felt like my opinion mattered and I could do something about the way my kids were being taught.

Bebo was an online social site that was big at the time and we would share the pictures of our nights out and would catch up with each other. It was amazing finding lots of long lost friends again. I had even managed to find my friend Nikki from my childhood in Dundee. I found other people from then also but I would just snoop on their pages, not wanting them to know who I was and where I was.

" We didn't know we were making memories, we just knew we were having fun"

Shannon was starting school and boy was she excited. A lot of her friends from nursery were moving up with her and were to be in her class. Katie and Lexi were the two that Shannon grew very close to, three of them becoming inseparable. Shannon had also become friends with the girl who lived next door to us. Lola was two years older than Shannon but she would come through to play with Shannon and for a long time they were quite good friends. She started going to the Rainbows with her friends which then led to her moving up to the Brownies and now the Guides that she loves.

It was Shannon's 5th birthday and finally her girly side was coming out of her. She wanted a princess party and invited all her girlfriends. I converted my living room into a pink haven for little girls with a princess blow up castle to play in, lots of pink decorations and streamers, kids pink champagne in pink plastic champagne flutes with strawberries and every girl came dressed as their favourite Disney princess.

When it came to Katie's party Nancy hired a pink limo for the girls and only Nancy and I got to accompany them. It was the first time I had been in a limo, was a great laugh. It was on Kacy's 30th birthday that we decided to all chip in and surprise her with a trip out in a limo before hitting the pubs. We arranged to have drinks at her house where we sorted ourselves out, did our hair, lashes etc followed by her surprise of the limo parking right outside her house to pick us up. What a laugh that night was, hanging out the sunroof touring around town, ducking back in whenever we seen the cops, champagne flowing, pub crawls, karaoke, not by myself I must add as I'm tone deaf, then finishing off in a nightclub for a good old dance, great times and a load of fun memories. We did the same for Keira's 40th birthday.

I just loved parties whether they were for the kids or for the adults. I soon began making up for all the birthday parties I hadn't had when I was a child. I would put my heart and soul into planning the parties for Shannon and Jack and loved to be involved when it came to any kind of event with the parent council or for family and friends. I held cocktail nights, Ann summer nights, candle parties, Body shop parties as well as the kid's parties. Mum and my cousin Charley would usually join us on such nights and boy did we have a great laugh.

"Maybe there is more that we all could of done, but we just have to let the guilt remind us to do better next time" _Veronica Roth

Mark and the kids had been at me for some time to get a family dog to complete our wee unit and to start with I wasn't convinced. I had grown up with dogs when I was younger but it had been a long time ago and Mark's parents had always had dogs. We looked at different breeds and fell in love with the beagle. I still wasn't sure until we went to see a breeder and I instantly fell in love. A few weeks later we went back to collect a tiny lemon bitch which we called Bonnie. She was a pedigree pup with beautiful markings on her head and body. The kids loved her, Jack was still very young and would tease her but Shannon had always loved dogs and now she had her own.

For a while it was ok but she was a puppy and we hadn't properly thought about how hard it would be to train her. I was the one who wasn't 100% sure about having a dog and it was me who ultimately ended up having to look after her. Shannon was at school but also too young, Mark was at work all day and Jack was still a toddler. I didn't have a clue what I was doing. Being a puppy she would chew and bite on anything she could get a hold of, would latch onto your feet as you walked past her. It was funny at first but soon I grew tired of it and she would bite the kids who were too young to defend themselves. She didn't mean it in a malicious way as really she was just playing but her teeth were sharp and she loved to nibble on Jack. Then there was the constant dribbling of pee everywhere when someone came into the house. It was just an excitement thing but I was constantly running around cleaning up after her. It was the pooing all over the kitchen every night that was the worst. We would come down stairs every morning to either piles of poo everywhere or the horrible smell of it but it was gone as she had eaten it. I was completely disgusted by it. I had a dog that liked attention and wanted kisses all the time but she was eating her own poo and the thought of her kissing me or the kids turned my stomach. There was also the issue of the grass dying in the back garden as her urine was killing it, I would have to check our entire garden for poo every time the kids wanted out to play and the neighbours had complained about her barking. We tried for a few months but after so long and no change Mark and I sat down to decide what we were going to do. I had recently started a course to train as a childminder and I was starting to learn that having a dog with Bonnie's characteristics was in no way going to be acceptable while caring for other people children in my home.

I had for several months wanted to go back to work as I needed some independence, would lie awake at night racking my brain of what to do with my life. I loved cooking and had started learning stuff off my own back through study books and cookery books. I thought about doing a catering course but it was never going to happen as the college hours weren't suitable with two children and Jack was still too young to go to their creche. I thought about a cleaning job, just a few hours to give me something to do but again most of them consisted of starting early morning, long before Shannon started school. I had heard stories from Skylar about her childminding job and thought it sounded perfect. We met up and she gave me all the information I would need to get started up and the numbers I needed to get on the course. I think Mark was a little shocked at my decision but he was 100% behind me as he always was.

I did my 6 week course on childminding and got my disclosure sent away to await the pass or fail. I meantime did the courses that were also needed to be done before they would fully register me. They consisted of First Aid, Child Protection and food and hygiene. I had to wait several months and undergo a full home inspection as well as write out all my policies before I finally got my certificates. During this long process we had finally decided that Bonnie would have to go back to the breeder, I couldn't risk a legal suit on myself from her attacking someone else's child. Shannon was heart- broken and I was too purely from listening to my little girl cry herself to sleep at night.

It was Valentine's day when we all said good bye to Bonnie. I Held her in my lap all the way back to Fraserburgh and she was terrified. She was whining most of the way there and just before we arrived she peed all over me. It was as if she knew she was going back and it made the journey all the more heartbreaking. I kissed her fore head and handed her to Mark who was welling up as he handed her to the breeder who instantly carted her off to the kennels, I just couldn't watch. The journey home was a sombre one and later Mark and I went out for our Valentines meal and reflected on what we had just done. Had it been the right thing to do? As heart wrenching as it was we knew deep down we had done the right thing. The kids were at grannies to be away from what we were doing but Shannon knew fine well what was happening and it took a long time for her to get over it.

When I finally got all my certificates through I was over the moon. All my friends had known that I was about to start childminding so when I finally passed, Kacy approached me asking If I would look after Kitty and Ronnie for her. It was ideal as they were brother and sister so I would get payment for them both and it would be easy enough for me to get started up. The only problem was that Skylar was currently minding Ronnie while Kitty was at playgroup. Now that she was getting older she needed to go to a childminder like her older brother and Kacy knew Skylar didn't have space for her. I had no children and Kacy knew that she didn't have to worry about putting the kids to two different people. It put me in a very awkward position at the time and I know Skylar wasn't very happy with us but I was trying to get work and she had it coming out of her ears. I did talk to her about it before signing any contracts but even though she said she was fine I just knew she wasn't.

I loved having Kitty and Ronnie. It was almost like having an extended family unit, like I had 4 kids instead of two. I didn't have them all day unless it was the school holidays but had them most days after school and nursery and I put everything into making sure they were entertained and learning. Jack was still at home all day with me so he loved having them over, he would have someone to play with and he was getting to do all sorts of things that he hadn't done before. I would organise all sorts of arts and crafts, baking and cooking, games and puzzles, stocked up on dressing up and role playing toys and equipment for them to play with, in our large back garden. When I wasn't working and playing with the kids I was up late studying online and researching for new things to do. I started studying child development off my own back so that I was getting an insight into what the kids were learning through our play and would incorporate self esteem activities and praised them as often as possible. Possibly looking back it was my way of making sure they didn't turn out like I had.

"Wisdom is not a product of schooling but of the lifelong attempt to acquire it" _*Albert Einstein*

It was Jacks 3rd birthday and he was mad about Bob the builder and Handy many so I decided to throw him a party with a construction work theme. We had gotten tickets to take him to Glasgow to see Bob the builder live which was brilliant. I blocked off one of the doors in the living room to put in a construction themed ball pit which I placed handmade tools for a game I invented. Instead of pass the parcel it was pass the brick and they had wheel barrow races. I filled up a second ball pit with hundreds of Duplo blocks for them to build stuff and had construction work decorations all over the room. It was a great party but sadly Jack can't remember it. At least he has the photos to look back at. I just loved organising parties and having the extra company.

Then it was Halloween and with all our new found friends I decided to hold a Halloween party at the house. I went crazy buying loads of Halloween decorations, making the house look like one of those American houses at that time of year. Mark didn't know the half of what I had spent. We had carved pumpkins, webs with spiders on almost every surface, scene setters on the walls, glow in the dark objects in the hall with hundreds of bats hanging from the ceiling making it look like a bat cave. I bought black roses with blood on them for the vases, a giant cardboard cut out of a haunted house, and had stuff all over the walls in every room apart from the bedrooms. I removed the normal light bulbs from the lights in the hall way and replaced them with red ones to make an eerie effect.

As for the food I made hundreds of stuff and named it all with scary names. The plate of smoked salmon was zombie flesh, I made ribs and steak bites with my homemade extremely spicy bloody mary sauce that was body parts with blood complete with blood soaked toy knife and fake organs. The kids drink fountain was green with floating eye balls and the dipping chocolate for the fruit was coloured green to look like slime and put in a heated cauldron. These were only a few of the many things I made. I put my heart and soul into the whole thing doing it all by myself. I even made time to make my very first decorated cake.

I baked a cake then carved it to look like a coffin, baked another and carved it to look like a cauldron decorating them on one large board and making ghosts, skulls and pumpkins out of icing and placing them on and around the cake. There wasn't a single person that didn't compliment me on my efforts and my cake and it made me feel great about myself.

I 'm sure if my house had been a nightclub we would of been closed down due to over capacity, there was so many people there that night and everyone made an effort to dress up. Mark and I were male and female pirates, Shannon was a red devil and Jack was Lightening Mcqueen from the Disney movie Cars. I had a blow up drinks cooler in the shape of a giant coffin with a skeleton coming out of it, filled to the brim with drink. I made vodka jello shots and punch which was served in my new skull punch bowl with a floating ice hand in it. It was a fantastic night in all and everyone was speaking about it for a long time afterwards.

After the success of the cake I had made for the Halloween party I decided to make a birthday cake for my dad in December. It was his 50th birthday and I made a 2 tier cake with a baking theme to represent his baker career when I was a child. I also made a cake in the January for my mother in laws 60th making it to look like a box of chocolates. I was a perfectionist and these cakes were far for perfect and it bugged me. I wanted them to be perfect but just didn't have the knowledge. Skylar asked me to make her 40th birthday cake and she would pay me. It was the first time someone had offered to pay for my work and it was an honour to do it. For her to believe in me to be able to produce one for a party that everyone would be at and to pay me for it was a turning point for me. I then decided to read up on cake decorating to try and learn what I was doing so to do it properly.

"Life is not about waiting for the storm to pass, it's about learning to dance in the rain."

We were finding that we weren't using the caravan as often as before and it was simply because it was getting too small for us. We wanted to get a new one but didn't have the funds. Marks parents offered to loan us the money so between that and the sale of the caravan we currently had we soon had the funds to get a bigger one. Mark had wanted a car with a diesel engine so when we had moved into the home we were in we traded the Mazda in for a Vauxhall Vectra so he had more than enough power to tow the larger caravan.

I loved getting away with the caravan even if only for the one night. We had been to Ayr with the previous caravan which resulted in an A&E visit for Shannon after she fell off the bunk bed banging her head, up north to visit family which almost resulted in an A&E visit for Shannon as she had fallen ill and was having convulsions with her high temperature and locally just to get away for the night. We had also been to Pitlochry, had gone up with Dillan, Kate and the kids. Jack was a baby at the time and he was a screaming nightmare. After a few nights away we had to get Marks mum and dad to come and collect him so that we could continue with our holiday with our friends in peace. We had planned to stay at Pitlochry for a week then move on to Comrie for a few nights. I felt terrible handing Jack over but it was a living nightmare being stuck in such a small space with a teething baby. The holiday had been far from relaxing.

We all went to a place called Landmark on the A9 not far from Inverness and Dillan and I decided to go on this thing were you climb up a tall log to a platform high above everyone and basically throw yourself off it. It had a harness on it with a cable that broke your fall just as you were about to hit the ground but it was scary as hell. I have no idea why I wanted to do it but it was just a spur of the moment decision that made me feel great. What a rush, I was scared of heights which made it all the more strange why I wanted to do it, standing on the edge of the platform which was only about a metre square, nothing to hold onto and just leap off. There were a few people that chickened out once they got up there, sitting on the edge rather than standing with their feet dangling off the edge, having to be rescued.

Now that we had a larger caravan it was time to start going away again. We took it to a site just outside a place called Story Book Glen for Easter. We also went to Loch Lomond which was probably one of my favourite sites from all we had been too. We weren't too far away from my relatives up in Kinlochleven, managing to visit them for the day. There was beautiful scenery all around us and we took a trip in a boat up the loch. I hated boats and was petrified of deep water but I faced my demons and did it for Mark and the kids. I won't be doing it again in a hurry though. I think this was one of the only longer trips in the caravan that we didn't have any hiccups. Our very last trip was a two night stay at the Truckfest in Edinburgh.

It all seemed like a good idea at the time but proved to be a nightmare. We had been going to the Truckfest every year since Mark and I had met and loved it. One of the very first times I went, I got a helicopter ride which seemed like a great idea just like the drop at Landmark and was also a spur of the moment decision. I was sitting at the end of a small group of people and had floor to ceiling window at the side of me. At take off it wasn't too bad but as soon as the pilot turned tilting the whole helicopter, my stomach ended up in my throat. I was desperate to get off and couldn't. It was a ride that will never willingly be repeated.

We loved to watch the Monster trucks at the Truckfest, smashing up the old cars but once Shannon was born had to keep our distance as the first time she saw them she had been on her dad's shoulders and as soon as they started revving up, vibrating through our feet she wet herself soaking Mark and herself.

We even visited the Truckfests in England. One was when we were on holiday in the Yorkshire dales and the big one was at Peterborough. The first time I went to the big one was when I was pregnant with Shannon. I must off been about 6 months gone and was feeling quite good, had walked about all day then travelled home late that afternoon.

The night before was hard as the room was so hot and the air conditioning wasn't working and being pregnant I was like an oven anyway. Then the next day wandering about in the sun I got sunburn. I loved going though and it was worth the long journey. We went back when jack was a new born baby, taking my Mum and Dad with us to help out.

It was on this last trip with the caravan to Edinburgh that changed my whole perspective of the event. We un hitched no problem and went for a wonder around the park, even dumped into Rick from the tv show 'Ice road truckers', just casually wondering about with a bottle of beer, posing for pictures and autographs from visitors. It turned out that Mark knew the guys staying next to us and several others that were down for the weekend. That was to be expected but it was the way Mark acted that disgusted me. I didn't have a problem with him having a few drinks with the boys but he was on holiday with his family, it wasn't a boy's party weekend. He went out for a few drinks which I didn't mind but he didn't come back.

Once it had got late I tried to contact him to see when he would be back, I didn't want to lock the door for him to have to wake us all up and didn't want to leave it open as there were hundreds of people wandering about and I was alone with two young kids. His phone was switched off and I grew frantic with worry which turned to anger then to fear when there was still no sign of him the next morning. I had barely slept a wink all night, couldn't go out looking for him as the kids were sleeping and there were parties going on all over the park. He was eventually found sleeping in the back of some guys car, had been off his head drunk and no recollection of how he got there. Both of our parents were coming down for the day and we had to entertain them. At the time I couldn't be bothered, was feeling ill with lack of sleep and worry but looking back I'm thankful they came down as if it wasn't for them I probably would of killed him. It was ultimately the last trip in the caravan as I was starting to feel like it was jinxed.

" It doesn't have to be the last good time. But sooner or later the last good time would come around." _Steven King

I was really enjoying my job looking after Kitty and Ronnie, invited them to Shannon's High school musical themed party. I had hired a hall this time, had a bouncy castle, basket ball nets and blow up musical instruments and a stage for the kids to act out their favourite scenes from the movie. They all loved High School Musical at the time and would sit about signing the songs when together. I made a small cake playing about with cake decorating again but still not getting it the way I wanted it to look. It was on Jacks next birthday that I started to understand a bit more about it. I decided to make a 3d Fireman Sam truck cake to match his choice of theme. He was mad about Fireman Sam, had all the vehicles that we had managed to get for him going around the car boot sales. We had the party at home and we hired a fire truck to take the kids for a tour. It was amazing to see all their little faces when it turned up at our front door. Even little Liam came. Liam was another little boy that I had taken on, on a full time basis so Jack now had a full time friend to play with each day while Shannon and the others were at school. He was a sweet little boy but always played up for his mum Summer. Summer and I went to school together but hadn't kept in touch. We started catching up again and reminiscing about people once I had taken on the job of watching Liam. She became a good friend and I felt comfortable looking after Liam for her so she could go back to work and college.

In the summer months I would have everyone over for parties in the garden and days lounging about on the deck chairs. Josh, Marks dad and I had dug out the garden when we first moved in, turned it from an old looking allotment to a safe place for the kids to play. I had borrowed my Dad's pick axe and a strong shovel to dig out a few large tree trunks, didn't mind getting my hands dirty. We laid the bottom half of the garden in play bark and the rest was grass, perfect for them pitching up their play tents and bouncing about on space hoppers.

Jack loved his ride in vehicles from his little tykes car, his tractor, ride in Fireman Sam truck and a Daf truck. He hated it when anyone was to go in one of them and had to learn to share pretty fast. I always held the end of term party at mine to celebrate the kids coming off for the summer. We would all get together to produce the food and drink and I supplied the space. We would get the swimming pools out, the loungers and barbeque. The kids would run about daft while us mums sat back with a glass of wine and chatted about anything and everything. One year I decided to turn the party into a Carnival party and got the kids involved through the childminding. They made invites and we discussed games and foods etc that we could use. I wanted them to be as hands on with the event as possible. It was the best party yet. We had everything from face painting, hook a duck, wet sponge throwing and even carnival mirrors that make your body look all wonky. I collected old tin cans and made a tin-can alley and a coconut shy, made up coin tossing games and had a dart board with balloons on it to pop. We had a bouncy castle and all the kids got coins to use on all the games winning tokens to use on the lucky dips at the end of the day for prizes.

All the mums chipped in and helped out. We ended up with a candy floss machine which went down a treat with all the kids as did the bags of popcorn that we made up. It was always a great time for the kids when we had our parties in the back garden and was the perfect opportunity for us mums to get together and have afternoon drinks and a laugh while our men were still at work. We didn't always exclude them though, on this occasion we had the party on a weekend so that it could be a family day. Mark never minded me drinking in the afternoon with the girls. He would come home, crack open a beer and join us in the sun out the back door. He never complained when his house and garden was a mess, always knew it would go back to normal. I loved that about him, he was laid back about it all and always really supportive about my crazy ideas.

I liked to organise days out when I was working, this was usually when the kids were on school holidays. I did on the odd occasion take them to the library or the park but when we had more time I would take them down to the beach front and take a picnic. I liked to take them to Jumping Joeys an indoor kids fun park but because I don't drive we would have to walk the 45mins to get there meaning we would have to have more than just a few hours to go. The kids loved it there and I took that into account when Red nose day was approaching. I decided that I wanted to do something for the charity through my work with the kids. We would do something with the school every year when I was growing up, whether it was dressing up, sponsored silences or the likes. I remember it being fun and I wanted something for my kids to remember.

I decided to organise a walk from the school to Jumping Joeys on the beach front. It was a 45 minute walk for us adults but with little kiddies in tow it was longer, was quite a distance for a little one to walk. I named the event' Walk in Red', contacted the BBC to get my fundraising pack with all the sponsor forms for the kids. Some mums and their kids wanted to get involved as well as a couple of other childminders. I got the kids to make banners and decorate money collecting buckets, we all wore red and our red noses and walked down after school finished. All the kids were chanting and having a laugh on the way collecting pennies from shoppers as we passed through the High street. The local paper turned up to take our picture before we went on our way and then when we arrived at our destination the kids spent 2 hrs running around daft inside, their wee treat for doing the walk and raising the funds. We raised near £400 and I received a signed t shirt from Keith Lemmon for my efforts.

In the summer I liked to have picnics with the kids whether it was just in the garden or down at the beach. Nancy and I had grown close and she would come around often when I was working and all the kids would play together. We had decided to go down the front on this particular occasion, took a football and a basket of food and some blankets. We had not long arrived at the beach front when I got a phone call from my Dad which was unusual as he never called my mobile. He was on edge wanting to know where I was, told me we needed to go through to Dundee as Grandad was dying. Dying!!! I told him where I was and I began to panic, I had a pile of kids with me and there was no time, Dad was on his way to get me. God knows what I would of done without Nancy that day as she took all the kids back to mine in a mini bus and awaited their parents collecting them explaining it was a family emergency.

We rushed through collecting my Gran on the way from the care home she was currently in for respite. They had both been in separate respite care homes when my Grandad had taken ill and was rushed to Ninewells hospital. Walking hurriedly along the corridor to the ward he was in was almost like a nasty dream where you never seem to get to where you need to be, when the corridors grow longer and narrower. We reached his room and just as we were about to step inside a nurse stopped us and asked us to follow her to the family room. This couldn't be good! Why weren't we allowed to see him? He was already gone and they wanted to prepare us before seeing him.

I was devastated, not only for myself but for my Dad who had lost his father and for my Gran who had lost the love of her life. He was lying there all peaceful, a shell of a man he once was. He had lost so much weight and his mouth was drawn in because his false teeth had been removed. I had never seen a dead body before. His skin was all shiny with a waxy feel to it and a yellow tinge of colour. I held his hand and kissed his forehead and quietly said goodbye as everyone stood by and waited their turn to do the same. It was watching my dad break down that got me. Seeing someone in so much pain and watching my Gran be so strong, it had me breaking in two.

The funeral that followed was hard. I had never been to a funeral of a loved one before, had never been up front in the family section. I felt like all eyes were on us and all I wanted to do was break down.

I never broke down in front of anyone and was trying so hard not to do it now. When the coffin went down to the pits of the crematorium my Dad broke down and my body started to rumble inside as I tried so hard to contain my emotions. Mark held my hand tight his love getting me through it. I adored him for being there for me. He had never had to be there like that for me before. He was my rock.

"Tears are the words the mouth can't say nor can the heart bare" – *Joshua Wisenbaker*

"Gone-flitted away, taken the stars from the night and the sun from the day! Gone, and a cloud in my heart" _Alfred Tennyson

Chapter Twenty Two

It was hard watching Gran deteriorate after Grandads death. She had lost the love of her life and had to move into a care home permanently to get the care she needed. In order to pay for her care she had to give up her savings and sell the family home to cover the mounting depts. I hated the thought of her being in there all alone without family, neighbours and care workers constantly looking in on her. The heart of our family was being sold and it was an end of a very long era.

I just couldn't imagine loosing Mark after being married for 60 years then having to move out of what had been our family home for over 40 years, into a place full of strangers and being incapable of going where I wanted and when I wanted. It hadn't seemed that long since all the family came together for the celebration of their 60th wedding anniversary. Little did we know at the time that it was to be the last time we would all be together for such a happy occasion. What came next was to be family gatherings celebrating the lives and mourning the loss of our loved ones, the end of an entire generation.

I would visit when I could, would tag along with Dad every week through to Dundee bringing along the kids when they weren't at school or nursery. I had being going through regularly on my days off from work with Dad since I was a teenager. We would take Gran to Tesco for a weekly shop up until she was unable to go with us then she would write us a list of what she wanted and needed. Dad would collect Grans pension for her, head to Tesco's for the shop then on our return we would have something to eat and I would set about doing anything around the house that was needed doing, cleaning, ironing, hanging curtains, sometimes painting and helping with her personal hygiene. There had come a time when Gran eventually couldn't get up out of bed to spend time with us around the house, in the kitchen cooking, in the living room having a cup of tea or in the garden pottering about. We would sit with her in the bedroom and tell her stories of what was happening in our lives and Grandad when not in respite care would join us.

Visiting Gran in the care home each week was hard and through time although I loved her dearly I dreaded it a little. I would sit in her little room and talk about what her great grandchildren had been up to and what was happening in our own lives. She would get a little confused at times referring to Grandad as if he was still here with us and would often ask when she was getting to go home and it broke my heart.

One week while visiting, Dad's brother, Uncle Sam had been there and had commented about how he had been up to the house and it had been cleared out. Aunt Jessica had been up and cleared it all out, preparing everything for the house going on the market. "And I have nothing" was Grans reply. In that moment my heart almost stopped from hearing the pain in her voice.

After leaving the care home and enduring the heart wrenching visit Dad and I went up to the house as Dad still had his keys. Nothing could prepare me for what I was about to walk into. The house was almost completely bare, most of its furniture gone. All the pictures were off the walls and piles of filled black bags were lying about in each room and on the stairs. My childhood sanctuary was no more.

I had asked Gran if it was possible if I could have the coo coo clock that once chimed from the living room wall but it had been chucked on top of a pile of black bags filled with rubbish with one of its hands broken off. It had long since stopped working properly but to me it was sentimental. It still to this day has pride of place on my living room wall.

The original wedding photos which I had used to make copies for a scrap book for Gran and Grandad for their 60th wedding anniversary were gone, I wanted to be able to take them up to Gran to cheer her up, to remind her of the good times we all had not so long ago when we were all together as a family for the last time. I never found out where they ended up but at least I knew that Gran still had the scrapbook. There was a small pile of family photos that Mum and Dad had given to Gran and Grandad, of the family when I was younger and old photos of Dylan and me from school. I gathered them up and put them in a box to take home, later using them to make up a second scrapbook for Gran to browse through when she was feeling lonely, as there wasn't enough room in her new home to have them all hanging on the wall. This was the next best thing.

Dads sister, Aunt Jessica was 10 years his senior. She had been clearing out Grans attic throughout the years and I hadn't known about it. The attic had been a treasure trove and I had spent many hours up there as a child playing, shelves full of trinkets and dishes, wardrobes full of old fur coats, old cameras, drawers full of sheets and clothes, Dads old book shelve full of his books from his childhood and Dylan and I's books for when we were younger, board games, coin collections, old baseball and football cards, an old work bench with car parts, Dad's old skiing stuff and an old trunk full of vintage Victorian dresses than Gran had once got me as a child for playing dress up. It reminded me of one of my favourite films as a child, 'The Goonies'. It was a space full of treasures where I loved to rummage and play out the make believe stories in my head.

It was all gone.... but while rummaging through rubbish bags and boxes I gathered up a few bits and bobs that I just could not let the bin men take away. 'One man's rubbish is another man's treasure' and in this case it was true. I had managed to salvage amongst the rubbish some little trinkets that once sat in a display cabinet in the living room along with some old books that were mine as a child, a tin of old marbles that I would play bagatelle with as a child and the biggest treasure of all was a huge pile of diaries, Grans diaries going way back into the 1960's. Over the coming months I sat and read them, I got a glimpse of what it was like to walk in the shoes of my idol and learned that she could write poetry. Most of the poetry was about life and God as Gran was a religious person but now I knew more about her creative side and where I got my abilities from. I dream to one day publish them in memory of her, possibly even collaborate them with some of my own work.

"When the snows fall and the white winds blow, the lone wolf dies but the pack survives." _George R R Martin

Chapter Twenty Three

Jack was now starting nursery and settling in was proving to be a complete nightmare. He was a mummy's boy at best and he just didn't want to be away from me, the polar opposite to Shannon when it came to starting nursery. He had slowly started learning to share his toys and play games with other children with me now being a childminder but when it came to leaving him in the capable hands of the nursery staff he would hang on to my leg with a death grip and scream the place down, making his face go bright red soaking not only himself with real tears but also myself and it killed me.

The nursery staff told me to walk away and not look back at him. I would have to just leave him and let them deal with the aftermath and often he wouldn't even look at me when I came to pick him up which broke my heart. I hated that I was putting him through this but deep down I knew it was what had to be done. He would hang onto the wall, hide his face in the corner and scream for me and as I walked out the door he would come running for me. It got so bad that eventually they asked me to get someone else to walk him in each day so that it was easier for them. I would collect him so that he would eventually come running to me smiling and wanting to show me what he had been doing during the session. Slowly day by day it got easier for us both, but it had been so hard as a mother to watch.

Nadine stepped up as the person to walk him each day as all of us mums were usually at the school gates anyway dropping off the older children for school. It was a god send and eventually it got easier watching him go which soon allowed me to drop him off myself when he had settled in properly. He became a much liked little boy and always had children around him wanting to play with him. Over the years that followed he became very popular, even with the older kids, walking down town they would say 'hi Jack' and I would be like 'who's that? ', 'oh just someone from school mum' he would say.

Madeline was the chair person for the parent council at the school of which I was still a member of and an assistant within the school the kids attended. She had a little girl at nursery with Jack and was looking for childcare for her. Emma was currently child minded by Skylar but Madeline had her disagreements with her methods and asked me if I would be willing to take her as her contract with Skylar was up for renewal. I was desperately needing the extra work with the depts that where slowly getting bigger and bigger but Skylar was my friend and it was hard to hear the things that Madeline was saying about her.

In the end it came down to the fact that I desperately needed the money, couldn't turn down the extra money. Jack and Emma had already gotten to know each other well through nursery, plus I had the bonus of walking them back and forth together for their nursery sessions instead of doing extra trips back and forth. I felt terrible doing it to Skylar again, taking on one of the children that were in her care but I was desperate. She would often go on about this child and that and the possibility of giving the whole thing up, wanting her home back and a normal 9-5 job. I may off ultimately been a big part in her decision making when she actually went through with it and got herself a normal job.

I knew deep down she wasn't really into it anymore, not like I was. I had grown dedicated to it and was eager to learn more. I started studying child development in my spare time, had spend hours at night reading and getting ideas together in hope of teaching the children and of doing the best by both my children. I knew Skylar wasn't happy with me when it happened, but when it did she held her tongue and eventually it was forgotten about.

Kitty and Ronnie continued to be in my care for months after I took on Liam and then Emma. It was fine as I would only have them and Liam after school hours on certain days which meant my day which was normally wasted doing nothing was now filled up with nursery runs and caring for Emma and Jack.

Kacy's marriage had broken down and I was shocked when she informed me. We had been friends for months now and she had to tell me in a formal way as I was also her childminder and had to know what was what for the continuation of the kids care. I felt put on the spot at times when the kids dad would arrive to collect them and she wanted to know all the little details which I was and wasn't to a point allowed to disclose. She became distant with me, started socialising with other people out with our little group and things became tense between us when it came to her paying up for my childminding services. She would avoid paying her bills would have other people either drop off or collect the kids so that she wouldn't have to face me. When she was around she would always have an excuse to not pay. I felt sorry for her and all that she was going through but I had bills too and ended up having to give her notice to terminate the contracts. It was horrible giving up Kitty and Ronnie as they had become part of the family and the kids loved having them around. After school hours wasn't the quite the same after they left, nor was childminding as a whole.

Slowly our nice little group of friends was getting smaller and smaller. Kacy had now distanced herself off from our group, had gone down a different route in life from the rest of us, Keira kept herself to herself a lot after suffering Breast cancer only occasionally catching up with the rest of us and now Tess was heading that way. She was single and at the time loving it. She got herself in a bit of bother with someone else's man, Lois's man to be precise. I didn't know him but Lois had become a friend of mine and a few other girls through the school gates and from being one of Nancy's old friends and neighbour. When Lois found out about what had happened you could say she went slightly loopy. She was mad and had good reason to be.

"Weak people revenge. Strong people forgive. Intelligent people ignore." *_Calvin Dillard*

By now almost everyone had a Facebook account online and used it for catching up with each other. Lois took to slandering Tess on most of the pictures that Tess had on her page and called her some very vile things. It was horrible to read and everyone could see it. Tess became isolated from everyone including us as a group but I never once didn't speak to her, would always remind her that she hadn't done anything to me so I wasn't taking sides with anyone. She knew she had done wrong and boy did she suffer for it. Then Lois turned on Nadine, started commenting on Nadine's marriage and they too fell out.

It was coming up for my 30th birthday and I had decided I wanted a birthday party, my first ever birthday party. I had started planning a Hollywood theme so that we could all get dressed up in outfits that we wouldn't usually get to wear, girls in long gowns and men in suits and kilts. With everything that was going on with our group of friends I hadn't invited Tess to the party because of the divide. She had done a horrible thing to Lois and I didn't want any agro at the party as it was all still so raw. I felt terrible not inviting her and explained that if I could have her there knowing it wouldn't kick of then she would be there but it was never going to be like that. As it was only days before my big day that Nadine and Lois had kicked off, I was then being told from a teary eyed Nadine that she wasn't coming either. She couldn't be held responsible for what might happen if they were both in the same room. It was sad not having them both there that night but it had to be that way.

It was my big day and I had planned everything down to the last minute. All my close friends and family met at our house where I was waiting all dressed up in my long red strapless gown. Nancy and the kids had come around as the kids wanted to get ready together and Nancy was curling and pinning my hair back, adding in some hair extensions to give it extra length and bulk. We were all ready dressed in our gowns, men in suits and kilts, Mark and Jack in the Royal Stewart tartan kilts, Shannon and I in red dresses, getting photos taken when the Hummer arrived. Mum and Dad had paid for us girls to all be collected and driven around town arriving at the venue in style. We had downed several bottles of champagne on route and were all high with excitement at the night ahead.

I had spent the whole afternoon decorating the hall with giant Hollywood signs, helium balloons, giant blow up Oscars and champagne bottle, stars hanging everywhere, stick on Hollywood walk stars on the floor leading to the bar, a giant cardboard cut out of an Oscar for getting your photo taking at and a red carpet complete with red rope and silver poles for arriving at the venue. It didn't stop there as I even organised the food with dads help. We had a sweetie buffet which I made up, a chocolate fountain with server paid by Nancy as a gift for my birthday, buffet food hot and cold prepared by me and Dad, a birthday cake made by Dad and I even made up sweetie favours for everyone in the shape of gold bars. I danced well into the night with the disco that I had paid for our evening's entertainment. Everyone had a brilliant night and I felt amazing. I had had my first birthday party to kick off my thirties and it had been in style.

It wasn't long after this that Lois started distancing herself from the rest of us, the ones she yet hadn't offended. Then she came to blows with Nancy and pushed herself away, became nasty towards us all. Between the quarrels between everyone I had never stopped speaking to Tess and Nadine, we would still see each other at the school gates and would go for breakfast or lunch down town. The falling out with Lois eventually brought the rest of us girls closer together than before. Lois started calling us the "Witches of Warddykes" behind our backs as we were always together at the school gates, Warddykes being the name of the school. All we could do was see the funny side of it and turned it around to be a positive thing. WOW then stood for Wonderful Outstanding Women. Becoming so close I designed a tattoo that I almost very nearly got on the back of my neck. Looking back now I'm so glad that I never went through with it. Something or another would come up and it would always get put on hold. I know now it was never meant to happen.

"Our anxiety does not empty tomorrow of its sorrows, but only empties today of its strengths." _Charles Spurgeon

Chapter Twenty Four

Things were great out and about when I was with the girls, we could have a laugh about anything and everything but at home things just weren't right and I couldn't put my finger on what it was. I was always feeling so lonely even when I had people around, I suppose working at home was a big factor in it but I just didn't feel myself. My Ibs was playing up and I always felt that Mark just didn't understand what it was and why I was the way I was. I remember writing an entry in my diary feeling so sad and fed up with life. I always spoke my mind in my diary and it helped me get out the feelings I was hiding inside. I never liked to show my emotions to others including Mark. I liked my privacy and hid a lot of things from everyone. I had written about how unexcited I was about life, that I just felt like a personal cleaner and a mum. I knew I just had to get on with it but felt that I didn't want to anymore. I wanted to be appreciated more from Mark and had considered asking him to move out for a while so that we could learn to appreciate each other more. Of course it never happened as I just couldn't speak the truth to anyone including Mark. I would bottle everything up inside and let loose in my diary. My diary had become my form of therapy.

I had been watching the news and the contraceptive pill that I was taking was getting a lot of bad reports. I had never taken into consideration what it was doing to my body as I had been on and off it since I was 15 years old and trusted it. When I started looking further into the prescription drug I soon realised that it may be a major factor in the way I was feeling. I had been suffering bad headaches for a long time and my libido was almost non -existent. Then there was the C word and that was it I no longer wanted to be on this drug because of the higher risk of developing Cancer. I spoke to Mark about my findings and decided I would come off the drug and we would take other precautions mainly condoms even though we hated them.

We had booked a holiday to Blackpool with the kids and it was the break that we both needed. I was starting to feel a bit better about life after coming off the contraceptive pill but I was really deluding myself to the fact that we were spending far too much money. I had won a holiday in a competition which landed on our wedding anniversary and we spend it in a luxury cottage with the kids down at Duchally only months after returning from Blackpool, which at the time had taken a big chunk of our money and of the credit cards. I had started feeling unwell while at Duchally and was struggling to keep down my meals at night. The heart burn was back but with a vengeance. It turned out that I had a stomach ulcer as well as a muscle that wasn't working properly meaning I would be on drugs for the rest of my life. Not only did I have reflux but after some tests they found out that I also had a nasty bacteria present in my stool which needed an urgent course of very strong antibiotics to kill it. I was told that if it was left unaided it could turn the stomach ulcer into cancerous cells. I had gone for weeks not knowing what was wrong with me, scared to go back to the doctors, was sick of the sight of the place but it really changed things for me when I finally did.

After my new medication kicked in my body was finally starting to feel normal again I had started to notice a huge difference in my moods. I was the happy go lucky me again and Mark and I's sex life hadn't been better. I was suddenly more aware of my sex drive and wanted more and more. With the lack of hormones blocking my libido from the contraceptive pill and the added risk from not being on it, I felt alive. I had never ever felt a feeling like it before, it had always been suppressed from the drugs stopping me from falling pregnant and in the past when I had deliberately stopped taking it I was in baby making mode. This was so different from before and I just couldn't get enough of the feeling. We both hated the lack of feeling when using condoms so occasionally we would risk it, Mark pulling out at the last minute, spilling his seamen all over my stomach, chest and back side when doing it doggy style. I loved it, he loved it. We just couldn't control ourselves.

Soon the sex was about the only good thing that was happening in our lives. We had decided to book a holiday to Euro Disney going by Euro star and staying at a Disney hotel for the kids Easter holiday treat. We told ourselves that money wasn't an issue but it was. We just put it all on the credit card. I had gotten a visa card for myself and when Mum and Dad were short of cash I let them use it to pay for a holiday for themselves thinking it wasn't a problem until Mum started struggling to pay it off, paying the minimum payment only each month. Mum, had always helped me when I needed it and I saw it as my way of being kind in return. She had also started using my clubby book for stuff around the house and Dylan used it for some over expensive computer. Soon my credit card was maxed out and clubby was almost maxed out and we were left with Marks credit card alone for stuff as our wages where barely paying off other bills.

Then Gran fell ill at the care home and we had to visit her in hospital being told that she could die. I was torn apart at that point as I couldn't bear to see her suffering. I recall standing in my bedroom trying to do the ironing to keep myself occupied before the kids coming home from school, head thinking a thousand thoughts, waiting for the phone call to say she had passed but instead a day later getting a call to say she was slowly on the mend. She was a fighter. That night while waiting on the phone call about Grans condition, not knowing what was happening, was she going to survive?, I received a drunken phone call from my Aunt Isa from up north telling me she had a knife to herself and was going to use it. Mark was working away over night that night and the kids were in bed. I was frantic with worry trying to get a hold of my cousins and my Uncle to make sure she was ok as I was over 100 miles away and could do no more. In the end she was ok, had apparently done this cry for help so many times at home as my Uncle couldn't apologise enough for her phone call. I was really upset with her that night. She had got me in the wrong frame of mind, not knowing what was happening with Gran. I didn't speak to my Aunt for a while after this, my head just had too much going on in it.

Then Summer was handing in her notice for Liam as she had fallen pregnant with her second child and would be off work, no longer needing my childminding services. Now it was down to only Emma for an income and Marks work was very quiet. The bills were coming in fast and we were struggling to cope. I started suffering from my Ibs on a whole other level than I had before. I started having panic and anxiety attacks. They became fierce sometimes hitting me without any warning and I couldn't cope.

Every morning I would wake and instantly need to be on the toilet, continued needing to go back and forth until early afternoon. It made it hard to go about my usual routine in the mornings as I needed to be by a toilet for hours. When leaving the house to take the kids to school and nursery I would feel my body go into a state of panic, my belly would start to churn and I would have to make my excuses at the gate to not hang around speaking with the girls, almost running all the way home so that I could be near a toilet. On the days when Dad and I were going up to Dundee to see Gran I would almost every time be sitting on the toilet right up until he arrived at the front door to pick me up. When I wasn't on the toilet waiting I was sitting on the back door step taking deep breaths in the fresh air as my breathing had become erratic and I was flushed with heat, my head in a spin as I struggled for breath. On route I would visually in my head be thinking of where would be the nearest point for Dad to stop so that I could go to the toilet and either be sick or release my bowels. I was fast developing a major physical and mental problem within my head and body.

I had stopped going out for breakfast with the girls in the morning because of my problem but if I was lucky I would see them for lunch. It was becoming rarer and rarer as the attacks once they had subsided left me feeling exhausted. I had completely drained my body of all energy and just wanted to sleep. The doctor referred me to see a psychologist about my problem. He explained to me that what I was feeling was panic and anxiety and he showed me how to deal with them, how to take the time to concentrate on my breathing. He explained the physics of the human digestive system to me to help me understand what my body was going through and how big a part my state of mind was playing on what my body was doing. I had to learn to relax and fight against the horrible thoughts that I had in my head. The tricks that I eventually got to grips with were what got me through the following months. Slowly I began to feel a little normal but still from time to time I had to remember what I was taught throughout our numerous sessions. I could go out and visit people again, slowly stopped panicking when we had to go out to visit relatives or do the shopping. I needed that even more so now that our holiday to Euro Disney was fast approaching and we had a long journey. Had I not gone to our sessions I would never of managed the trip, I had developed a fear of travelling because of my Ibs all though the anxiety and stresses that had slowly built up in my life.

Having unprotected sex was taken by a sudden unexpected surprise when I realised that I hadn't had a period for a while. At first I put it down to all the stress I had been putting my body through but now my breasts were becoming extremely sore. Really it was naive of me to think that our bedroom antics wouldn't go without consequence. Nancy came with me to the chemist where I bought a pregnancy test which soon after proved that I was indeed pregnant with baby number 3. I was completely shocked, at first didn't think I could do it all again. Mark felt the same and it didn't help when my Mum was acting along the same lines. She had sounded disappointed when I first told her but later got used to the idea as did we. Marks mum was all for it from the word go having had 3 children of her own and after having quizzed us about whether she would be a grandmother again or not.

I had always loved the name Jamie, loved the idea of possibly being able to use it should we have another son, in fact I was convinced we were having another son and I was determined to call him Jamie. We even started thinking about the living arrangements, which room each of the kids would have should it be a boy or a girl. I even went into the loft to see what we still had and didn't have from when the kids were babies to see all what we needed, making a list. I was 5 weeks gone when the morning sickness kicked in, again getting medication from the doctor to keep it in check and of course to help me on the long journey we were soon to be on as we left for Disney with the kids for Easter.

When I was 6 weeks gone I had a slight pink discharge in my pants that alarmed me slightly but the midwives said that it was sometimes normal for women to get this. I was very bloated by now so decided to tell the kids what was going on as well as the rest of the girls and Madeline, Emma's mum. Everyone was very excited for us all and the kids were over the moon that they were getting a little brother or sister. Shannon especially as she wanted to be the helpful big sister that she was too young to be when Jack was born.

I had recently started looking after Chloe, Skylar's younger daughter on a part time basis as she had gotten a new job and I was perfect for the job seeing the kids were all at school together. The extra money was a bonus but now I was pregnant I felt a little worried breaking the news to Skylar. Madeline, I wasn't worried about as Emma's contract was due to finish soon when the kids were to start going to school full time. I have no idea why I was worried as Skylar was over the moon for us. Being a good friend she was happy about it all. I was going to be the first person in our now close nit group of friends to have a baby. Of course we all had children but none of us were close when they were babies. This was going to be so special, had it all planned out in my head, I was going to make all the girls Aunties.

Gran had fallen ill again and we went up to visit her just days before we left for Disneyland. I was holding her hand telling her all about her going to be a great grandmother again and about our excitement for our holiday. She was delirious with the drugs and kept grunting and saying the word no! I have no idea if she knew that we were there that day or of what stories we told her. Aunty Jessica had to sign a DNR so that they wouldn't resuscitate Gran should her heart stop beating and it was all so much more real than the last time she had fallen ill.

Soon we got the phone call to say she had passed and my world fell apart. I was pregnant and hormonal as it was but this on top was breaking me in two. She was my idol, my second mother and no matter what anyone says, losing a grandmother like her was extremely difficult. I felt that none of my friends really understood what was going on in my head. To them she was just a grandmother. That I should get over it. I didn't know how I was meant to react to loosing someone I loved so dearly and I felt that I had no one to lean on for support. I felt that no one at that point truly understood what was going on in my head. I was so alone.

The family decided to postpone the funeral until after our holiday as they said that Gran wouldn't off wanted her great grandchildren to miss out on such a holiday having loved holidays herself. My only blessing now was the tiny bundle of joy growing within me. A soul was lost but another was flourishing.

"Turn off the light" she say as she walks away creating a small woosh that smells sweet and chemical. It makes me sad because it's the smell she makes when she's leaving" _Augusten Burroughs

"The loneliest moment in someone's life is when they are watching their whole world fall apart and all they can do is stare blankly."
_F. Scott Fitzgerald

Chapter Twenty Five

The trip to Disney land was a long one. It started via a train collecting us at Arbroath station that took us all the way to London where we stayed the night in a hotel, the next morning catching the Euro star direct into Disney land itself. In the days running up to the holiday I was finding myself out in the back garden on the swing listening to the music I had downloaded onto my I-phone. We were getting beautiful spring afternoons and I would sit and swing listening to my music with my headphones in, trying to come to terms with Grans death. I would rub my stomach, close my eyes looking up to the sun feeling its warmth through my eyelids, breathe in the fresh air and think about the gift that I had been given, the life within me. This child was going to be my god send. My saviour after losing someone I loved dearly. I was somehow going to incorporate Grans name Jennie into our unborn child's name even call her Jennie should I be wrong and end up having a girl instead of the boy I was convinced of.

I had recently downloaded a slow original version of a dance song that I loved as a teenager, 'Forever young' by Tiffany. As I swung on my swing with peace and quiet before Mark and the kids came home, I would weep as I listened to the words, imaging Gran as a young girl her whole life ahead of her, her body soon to be ashes, her soul now with the angels.

I was sitting on the train passing Edinburgh when the song came on and I held my breath so tight, lowered my head trying so hard to hold back the tears. I was quiet most of our journey, I couldn't express to Mark how hurt I was feeling inside, refused to let the kids see it. I didn't want to spoil what was meant to be a holiday of a life time.

The holiday was full of excitement for the kids. I should off been full of excitement too but I just wasn't feeling it. I was feeling sick with the morning sickness every morning and exhausted in the afternoons and all the while my heart was breaking. We stood in endless lines to get our photos taken with all the charters and Mark and Shannon went on numerous rides without Jack and I, Jack was either too little or too scared and I couldn't because I was pregnant. The few rides I did get on were great and it was nice to be having the family time but even the scorching sun couldn't lift my mood.

I had fallen for these two teddies in one of the gift shops while rubbing my expanding waist line, a Goofy and Donald duck teddy to put aside for our unborn child, their first gift. I wanted to get a family portrait done etched into glass while in the princess castle but Mark persuaded me to wait and come back after the birth to get a picture of our family complete with baby number three. We walked around all day in the beating sun and it was taking its toll on me. While visiting the toilets in one of the parks I noticed the discharge again, at almost 8 weeks but this time it was a little brownish in colour. I tried not to think about it but really with my state of mind I couldn't forget about it.

It was the 11th April 2011, the date Grandad would off celebrated his birthday had he still been with us and now it was to be the date we all mourned for Gran at her funeral. We had only been back a few days from our holiday and now the dreaded day had arrived, time to say our final goodbyes. I was now very bloated and looked pregnant so decided to tell the rest of the family at the wake. They were very pleased for us, for our little blessing in the wake of what had just happened. It was a very sad day, one I will never forget.

Two days later I had my booking in appointment with the midwife to go over all my vitals, history etc. They booked me in for my first scan to see my baby for the first time which would be in a few weeks time. I was so excited, rubbing my belly, counting my blessings.

I was almost 10 weeks gone now and really looking forward to seeing my baby in a couple of weeks. I had been feeling a bit off all day, felt very light headed and really sickly. There had been a little more discharge again but this time yellow. By night time the discharge had changed to brown and I was a little alarmed. I phoned the midwife who reassured me that I should be fine but booked me in for a scan the following morning just in case.

Mark had decided not to take the day off to come with me as we were both a little hopeful that everything would be ok, and we couldn't really afford for him to take the day off, so Dad took me up to the hospital instead and waited outside in the car for me. How wrong were we? If ever there was a time when I needed my husband most it was in the moments that followed.

Within minutes of entering the scan room my whole world came crashing down around me. I lay on the bed as the midwife began performing the scan only seconds later telling me that she was very sorry but it seemed that I had lost the baby. At first I was in shock, cleaned my belly of the gel and sat on a chair while the midwife left the room to make a phone call. At that precise moment when I was left alone, I broke. The room began to spin and seemed like it was closing in on me. I was all alone, nobody there to pick me up as I was falling, falling into a darkness that consumed me. I sobbed my heart out clenching my body with both arms, rocking back and forth on the cold plastic chair.

On the midwives return I tried to compose myself as she put her hand on my shoulder and asked if I was here with anyone? I explained that my Dad was outside waiting on me and that my husband was at work. She went on to explain that she had spoken to colleges at Ninewells hospital and that all hope was not lost. There was clearly still a sac in my womb and that there was a slight possibility that I was a lot earlier on in the pregnancy than first thought. She arranged for another scan in a week's time to see if there was any change, meanwhile I had to go home and rest. That was easier said than done and having to wait for a whole week to find out if I was still pregnant was just unthinkable.

Later that day I was standing outside the school waiting on the kids coming out when I started getting terrible pains in my stomach and back, shooting down into my legs. I wasn't bleeding but boy was I in a lot of pain. The hospital told me to rest as much as possible, that there was nothing they could do for me. I was to keep my scan appointment but meanwhile start taking pain killers and expect a lot of blood to follow at some point possibly later that day. By tea time I started bleeding but by bed time it had stopped again. The following days leading up to the scan I held onto the little hope I had that I hadn't lost our precious child. I still felt very much pregnant, I continued to be sick every morning and my breasts were still very sore and had already gone up a size.

11 weeks pregnant and I arrived at the hospital with Mark to see if there was still hope. At first they scanned me normally but couldn't get a clear view ending up having to do an internal scan. The scan that confirmed that I had indeed lost our child, my saviour was gone. My body wasn't excepting the miscarriage which was why I hadn't started bleeding like I should be and why the sac was still clearly attached inside my womb. The baby had either dissolved back into my body or had simply not developed in the sac.

It was the Friday before the Royal wedding and it was to be a holiday weekend with celebrations meaning that the hospital wasn't fully staffed. I would need to have surgery to remove the remains of the pregnancy but would have to wait another week to get booked in. I might be lucky and loose the remains while waiting but I wasn't so lucky. I continued to be in a lot of pain for the following week and still my body didn't reject the pregnancy meaning I had to go for the surgery.

I had spent the whole week mourning our loss and found it difficult to speak to people and to top it off I was now sitting in a ward full off women that were about to abort their pregnancies. I couldn't have Mark with me so he went to work as normal that day, had booked some time off to spend with me after it was all over. What didn't help with matters was when the surgeon asked while doing his rounds if it was a termination as in a planned one. That's when I realised I was amongst women who were getting rid of their perfectly healthy babies as they didn't want them and here was I sitting speaking to the surgeon explaining to him that I had no choice, that I had already lost the baby but the remains were still there.

The hours that followed were hard, was early afternoon before I was taken down to theatre. I had been given several suppositories in my back passage and in the front a few hours before hand to quicken the process and it worked. I was in extreme pain needing pain killers and I started to bleed very heavily. Eventually the porters arrived for me, I was asked to remove my underwear or the surgeon would need to cut them off but I opted to wear some disposable ones instead. I was carted down the long dark corridors on a bed then a needle was inserted into the back of my hand as I lay back and they placed a mask over my face making me drift off to sleep.

I was feeling all warm and happy, feeling blissful watching the kids run about in the back garden, the sun beating down on us as I swung back and forth on the garden swing. I was feeling such contentment. Then I was drifting, felt like I was waking up from a blissful dream in my own comfy bed until I felt the mask around my face. I opened my eyes looking around me to realise where I was. I was lying in a cold hospital bed with the sides up to protect me, an oxygen mask over my face and various drips and wires coming off me. I had come back down to earth with the cold realisation of where I was and what had just happened and all I wanted to do was curl up into a ball and weep.

A woman approached me and explained where I was and that I was ok, that I was going to be left there for a while until I came too properly. Then the pain came, it was a feeling almost like being in labour, so excruciatingly sore that I just wanted to tear at my body but didn't have the strength or energy to do so. The nurse administered some pain relief intravenously settling me for a while. Back in the ward I just wanted to sleep but found it difficult with the pain growing worse and the constant need to get the nurse to administer more pain relief. By tea time Mark arrived to bring me home and held me tight as I snuggled my hot water bottle as we lay on the sofa watching crappy television not knowing what to say to one another.

"Just like seeing that extra pink stripe on a pregnancy test, a miscarriage will change your life in an instant.

"I did the only thing I knew how to do: I built my own walls of silence to disguise my desperation and what later came to be recognised and diagnosed as depression." _Sharon E Rainey

Chapter Twenty Six

"Everyman has his secret sorrows which the world knows not; and often times we call a man cold when he is only sad." _Henry Wadsworth Longfellow

It was hard telling the kids what had happened, Jack didn't quite understand but Shannon got very upset. I suppose she had been really looking forward to being a big sister again. For days after the operation I went about my day in a complete daze. I would find anything and everything to do about the house to keep my mind occupied. Mark and Mum would be constantly be telling me to rest as my body was needing it after what had happened and they were right. I was making myself physically exhausted and the pain was a constant reminder of our loss. Friends would come and go, popping in for a cuppa and a hug but not once did I crack in front of anyone. I tried to hide my pain, I tried to stay strong even though inside a part of me was dying. I was sinking further and further into the pit of darkness that was consuming me.

I was losing interest in everything and everyone around me. Every time I saw a baby or heard one cry I would weep inside. I had spent a few weeks off from work to recover but once Emma started coming back to me I just didn't want her around me. I didn't want anybody's children near me. I completely lost all interest in being a childminder.

"The friend who holds your hand and says the wrong thing is made of dearer stuff than the one who stays away" _Barbara Kingsoliver

Going out for breakfast with the girls was a great distraction but I would sit and think about how everyone's life was moving forward yet mine felt like it had been frozen in time. Nancy was always complaining about this and that and I had lost my tolerance for her. I started getting snappy with her which eventually led to her distancing herself from me. I didn't really blame her for doing so but then I felt even more alone no matter how many people I had around me. I felt that if anyone understood what I was going through it would off been her, and she backed off when I needed her most. She had lost a little girl when she was a teenager, her birthday would off been on the same day that I had the operation, 3rd of May. I was naive to think that this would make us a little closer but I felt like it had pushed us further apart. I know it must of been hard, it all bringing back old memories for her but she was meant to be my best friend and she let me push her away.

"You're scared to tell people how much it hurts, so you keep it to yourself"

I would run myself a bath, lock the door and sit in it while it was still running and sob my heart out. Completely break down where nobody could see or hear my pain. I didn't want to be suffering anymore but I didn't know how to make it all better. I walked through life for the coming months as if I was standing still and everything else was whizzing past me at the speed of light. Was there no end to this pain?

"There are wounds that never show on the body that are deeper and more hurtful than anything that bleeds" _Laurell K. Hamilton

Money was at its lowest it had ever been and the bills were proving to be difficult to pay. Marks parents had previously given us a loan to buy a bigger caravan and started complaining when we were struggling to pay large sums back to them each month. We had no option but to sell our wee holiday home giving us enough to pay them back and pay off a few bills. I hated my work and had started dabbling into baking again after watching 'Cupcake wars' on television. It was a distraction to everything I was feeling inside. I would take cakes into the nursery to let the teachers sample and started trying to make decorations to go on them. Soon I was making larger cakes and managing to teach myself via magazines and you tube. Everyone would tell me that I had a talent and should sell them so through time I eventually decided that I was going to try and make a career out of it.

Dillan told me to set up a Facebook page and that I would be surprised at how much word of mouth would bring the business on. I was very surprised when people started placing orders. Before I set up my business page I had asked on my personal page on Facebook for people to suggest a business name for me. Marks Aunt from down south was the one who suggested the best name so on the 1st July 2011 'Mary Queen of Cupcakes' was established. I had done a lot of research and it wasn't much different from the childminding for my accounts. I contacted the Inland Revenue to register the business and got the Food standards agency to inspect the premises which was our home.

It was now the summer holidays so I wasn't childminding as with Madeline working at the school she had the holidays off too and didn't need me to look after Emma. I spend the summer investing time into my new business venture keeping myself and my mind busy. After the holidays Jack and Emma were starting school so I was only childminding in the afternoons. With Emma and Jack soon to be at school full time it meant that Emma's contract was soon to be running out and I hadn't bothered looking for other children to mind as my heart wasn't in the job anymore. I decided to give it up completely and work on my new business full time.

I had had to spend money that we didn't have to get the new business up and running and with me not having any steady work over the summer and Mark struggling to get overtime we were almost penniless. We had maxed out both of his credit cards, my card was still maxed out and we were failing to pay the mortgage and utility bills on time. It was starting to cause tension between Mark and I and we weren't sleeping at nights. We would argue over the silliest of things that would stem from the issue of money or the lack of it and I would constantly be moving this money and that money about trying my hardest to make what little we had work. I started selling unwanted or needed items from around the house making a good bit of money for all the childminding stuff that I no longer needed. Still it wasn't enough and any attempt at applying for a loan was refused. I pleaded with a woman at the bank to help us but they said there was nothing she could do for us. If something didn't change fast we would lose everything including the roof over our heads.

"Feeling lost, crazy and desperate belongs to a good life as much as optimism, certainty and reason" _Alain de Botton

Now that my body was healthy again, all I wanted was to be pregnant. Through all the organising of the new business and the money issues Mark and I had started trying for a baby again. I knew deep down that it was probably a bad idea seeing that we didn't have the money but it was all I could think about when it came to Mark. Having been pregnant not so long ago and remembering the excitement the news had first stirred up between us both, it was what I craved again.

I couldn't talk with the kids about our recent trip to Disneyland and couldn't look at the photos for the heartache it brought. In the pictures of me you could see the little baby bump and it hurt way too much. The Donald duck and Goofy that I had bought for our baby sat on my dressing table and I would hug them when nobody was around. I needed so desperately to be pregnant again and wanted it to happen to take the heart ache away.

Sex became a chore more than a pleasure. It was solely for the purpose of making a baby. I started buying ovulation tests from the shop to try and make it easier to fall pregnant and stocked up on tests just in case. Every month I would use them and each time be disappointed with the results. I even started going to the doctors to get my hormone levels tested which showed that the levels were fairly low but the possibility wasn't out of the question. Looking back now I was under way too much stress with our financial situation and putting too much pressure on us both the get pregnant for it to happen naturally.

I by chance received a phone call one day from a 0800 number which usually I would ignore but on this occasion I answered. It was from a company wanting to consolidate all our depts. A company called 'Credit Fix '. They were one of the companies linked to a new television advert that was currently always on, to do with the Scottish trust deed. At first I wasn't convinced, thought there must be some sort of catch. I got Mark to speak to them and because we were both at a point of desperation we arranged to have a meeting with them.

We had to take every dept we had and consolidate them. Consolidate everything from all the credit cards, store cards, clubby's and also the overdraft that I had maxed out when I was an art student. In total it came to something like £28,000, a hell of a lot of money when you put it all together like that. We would have to declare everything, release any equity in the house of which there was none, and sign up for 3 years paying them a set amount of money each month based on usual monthly income and expenditure we had. We had to supply proof of all this of course and were to do so on an annual basis. It was all too good to be true!! That one phone call that I had, on that occasion decided to answer led to the answer to our prayers.

With some of the dept being Mums with her maxing out my cubby and credit card we agreed for her to help with the payments until all her costs were paid off, pay us £100 each month to go towards our £300 a month bill. During the 3 years we would be allowed no credit what so ever, not even a new mobile phone contract. Afterwards if there was any equity in the house it would be released and the remaining depts would be wiped clean. Then it was up to us to build our credit rating back up from the black hole it was in.

Once the final papers were finally signed in the November, for the first time in months I got my first proper night's sleep where I had the most amazing dreams. We could now look forward to Xmas with family having bought most of what we needed before we signed the papers. We could now look forward to the future. In January the trust deed became protected meaning that none of the creditors had protested it and that now for the next 3 years we were safe, the roof over our heads was going nowhere unless we failed to pay our monthly £300 bill.

Money still continued to be very tight even after Xmas had passed. The bills were getting paid on time and that was the main thing. I continued to sell items online and the new business was getting busier and busier. Mark was still struggling to get the overtime so all of my earnings were going towards the bills that his wages would usually cover. Luxuries were sparse, takeaways and pub lunches were now only for special occasions. I was rarely out for lunch or breakfast with the girls but sometimes they would be kind and treat me to my meal so that I didn't have to be left out.

We always celebrated at Xmas, all us girls. Whether it was a girly night out or a girly night in, we always came together for the night. This year though had been the hardest ever for me with loosing Gran and then the pregnancy and the money problems that followed, it had damaged me. Nancy was still being distant with me and made up some stupid excuse not to come to the Xmas night in at mine. It was the first ever time she hadn't made an effort for one of our nights. I brushed it off in front of the girls saying I wasn't bothered anyway as we weren't close anymore but I was gutted. I had made special cupcakes for all the girls with photos of us all on top of them, something personal, a gift from me. Nancy not only didn't turn up for the night in but even after she was told I had a gift for her she never made the effort. In the end the box of cupcakes ended up in the bin as they went off.

For a long time Nancy had been my hairdresser and had regularly cut and coloured my hair for me. I had so badly needed my hair done after the crappy year I was having but she would always keep coming up with excuses, never actually setting a date or time for me to get it done. She kept brushing me off and it hurt. Things between us were not as they were and yeah I was probably the reason as I had pushed her away with my depression but she should off fought harder to be there for me.

"Saying someone can't be sad because someone else may have it worse is just like saying someone can't be happy because someone else might have it better."

"It is in this darkness that I found all the light – somehow become so bright, a shooting star on a stormy night" _Coco J. Ginger

Chapter Twenty Seven

February 28th 2012 and although we were now in a secure trust deed money was still very tight. It was my 32nd birthday and Mum and Dad decided to treat us all to a nice family meal at the Portcullis restaurant just down the road from where we lived. It was a lovely meal, always was when you went there but it was the first time we had been out for ages and I was really looking forward to it.

The occasion was made extra special when both Dylan and I were given a white envelope each just after the desserts had been devoured. Dad loving the puddings joked with us, had asked us if anyone wanted any more pudding and thinking he was being serious I had replied 'no thank you, I'm stuffed'. That's when they took out the two white envelopes and handed them to both Dylan and I.

If it had just been me I would off thought it was just another birthday gift but inside was a load of cash, £1000 to be exact. The sale of Grans house had finally gone through and Dad hadn't told us. This was a little something of what was left from the estate and although Mum and Dad knew of our money problems, they told us it was for under no circumstances to go towards bills. We had to use it for fun. Wow, I had £1000 to use to treat our selves. You could say I was a little overwhelmed with the gift.

We decided to book a nice little family holiday down to Scarborough for Easter, a chance to put everything behind us once and for all. And while we were feeling optimistic we also decided to save up the coupons in the Sun newspaper to get a cheap caravan holiday for during the summer holidays. We were determined to have a better year.

It was the 1st June 2012 and I had just found out that I was pregnant again. I had forgotten about the need for a baby, had started to feel a lot happier with in myself. I had had a nice holiday down to Scarborough, the business was booming and we had our cheap Sun package holiday to look forward to. I was over the moon with the news, couldn't quite believe it so I nipped down to the chemist to buy a digital test to see how far on I was. It told me that I was 4 weeks gone, still very early but I was over the moon regardless. With all that had happened the last time I was pregnant my doctor told me that he would arrange for an early pregnancy scan to keep my mind at rest. The earliest they could do it was when I was 7 weeks gone so I still had another three weeks to wait.

At 6 weeks pregnant I had booked the day off work to attend Skylars's mother in law's funeral. She had died of cancer and Skylar was distraught. Mark came with me as he was good friends with Issac, Skylar's husband. We both knew Martha and were sad to hear of her death when it happened but the whole day I had spent suffering from cramps but tried not to worry as I had had a lot of pain at the beginning of all my pregnancies and I didn't want to make a fuss at the funeral.

Later in the week I went out for breakfast with the girls and had become more and more anxious when visiting the public toilets I noticed brownish staining on my pants. It was another full day later when I started getting really bad pains but although the discharge had stopped it didn't help the anxiety building up inside me when the midwife told me to just put a pad on and wait and see what my scan said the following week. It was happening again. I was miscarrying and again like the last time there was this little bit of hope that I had to cling onto. I felt like a fragile vase that had cracked, the slighted touch and I would shatter into a million pieces. I had to yet again wait it out to see what the scan confirmed in a week's time.

A few days later I started bleeding but it was different this time, within it contained tissue. That was the moment when I knew all hope was lost. My vase had shattered but somehow I felt different this time. I actually felt a sense of relief like a huge weight had been lifted off my shoulder. I no longer had to spend every waking minute of every day wondering if it was going to happen again, it had happened again. The worst thing possible in my mind had occurred but somehow I felt that the worst was over and now I could glue myself back together piece by piece. The only problem in my mind then was would they have to intervene again, would they have to put me to sleep again to have the remains removed? With our family holiday fast approaching I didn't want to have to cancel it for the inconvenience of more surgery. I wanted to forget as quickly as I could, I wanted to spend quality time with the children I had.

I would of been almost 8 weeks gone when I was back up at Ninewells hospital getting the scan to 1 confirm the miscarriage and 2 tell me if I needed to have the surgery again. I had lost the baby but I already knew that and like before the sac was still attached but the baby was already gone. With being earlier on than the last time, surgery wasn't an option so instead I could have a new procedure where they would take the remains out while I was still awake but I would need a very high pain threshold to get it done. I decided to get booked in for it as I didn't want to be suffering for weeks like the last time. They also booked me in for the tablet option just in case I changed my mind before the procedure. The tablets would make my womb contract more, inducing a sort of labour but they would have to be taken a day apart and I would have to travel up to Ninewells each day to get them. They also weren't 100% successful of emptying the womb. The midwife told me that next time they will prescribe me a higher dose of folic acid so to help the pregnancy stay stronger in the important first few weeks. It was at that point Mark and I looked at each other and I knew in his eyes that he couldn't do this anymore, I couldn't do this anymore either but I didn't have the heart to tell the midwife that we had given up.

Two days later I started bleeding and contracting by myself. Standing in the living room I suddenly felt wet down below so went upstairs to the toilet to check. Upon sitting down on the toilet a golf ball sized clot fell out of me along with a massive gush of blood. I should off been prepared for it but it came as a shock, a sudden rush to my head that made me feel dizzy. I reached for a sanitary towel then phoned the hospital. Tramadol was prescribed for the pain and I was told to wear a maternity pad. I had some left over from the last miscarriage but the maternity pad within minutes of putting it on was soaked right through onto my pants. I was bleeding so heavily that I had to sit on the toilet to let it flush out my system. I had never in my life seen so much blood and it made me feel weak and faint. I bowed my head and held onto the towel rail by the side of the toilet where I'd been sitting for what seemed hours. Eventually I got up and curled up into a fetus position on top of our bed and began to drift. In a dream like state of mind I lay on our bed, the sun beating in the window on top on me. Completely alone I felt warm like I was being cuddled by the arms of loved ones. Someone or something was taking care of me like an unseen energy full of love.

A few days later I was back up at Ninewells getting the scans to confirm that my womb had cleared out properly, scans of my ovaries also to make sure all was well. I was thankful now for it was finally all over.

"Such healing can occur through the sexual act with a person you love and trust if the two of you can stay with each other during your most vulnerable moments. You enter into a sacred space, this unknown territory, from which you'll emerge into new and unexpected states of being."
_Alexandra Katehakis

Chapter Twenty Eight

"Do not ignore inspiration, it's your guide to self discovery"
_E'yen A Gardner

We were on holiday in a nice little holiday park on the outskirts of Edinburgh. We had saved up all the tokens in The Sun newspaper for a cheap family holiday and it couldn't off been timed more perfectly. When we first arrived I had still been bleeding from the miscarriage but it was starting to tail off and Mark and I were feeling closer to one another than we had in a long time. We had spoken to one another about the miscarriages and Mark opened up to me. He couldn't watch me go through it all again, it was killing him. When he realised that I just didn't have the strength to do it all again either we came to an agreement that we would stop. No more trying for babies, sex was going to for now on be purely for the pleasure.

I had just previously before having the miscarriage started reading a book that everyone was talking about. It had been a very long time since I had read a book for pleasure, had always been some form of study book or another. 'Fifty shades of grey' by E. L. James was the book. It started to open a whole new world to me that I knew existed but didn't know enough about. It made me horny and made me crave sex on a level had never encountered before.

We were in our wee caravan, the kids were asleep in their rooms and we had earlier visited an Ann summers shop in Edinburgh. I was dying to try out spanking. I had learned about it while reading my book and told mark about it. I was more or less finished bleeding from the miscarriage and we were both horny, dying to try out the new riding crop I had bought. I was on my knees bend over on the sofa and he started to beat me with the riding crop. To start with it was sore and I thought to myself 'why on earth would anyone want to do this?' Then my back side began to burn with a warming sensation that lead straight to my groin making me anxious for more.

We started using condoms again for fear of getting pregnant and the fear of getting an infection with not long miscarrying. I wasn't allowed to go swimming for a while and had to watch what I was doing. We had joked about Mark getting the snip at first but soon he was making an appointment to get it done. It was the safest way forward now that our minds had been made up. My body had been through the mill and I wanted a break from all the chemicals I had been pumping my body full off while being on the pill. Mark stood up as a man and took the lead as my husband to make sure I would never have to go through all that I had been through ever again. It had helped a great deal when he could turn to Issac, Skylar's husband. He had had it done and said it was a breeze so we got the ball rolling and waited for the appointment to come through the post.

As we waited I continued to read the 'Fifty shades of grey' books, all three of them. By the time they ended I was hooked on sex. My eyes were well and truly opened to the possibilities that waited in the bedroom.

"Man cannot discover new oceans unless he has the courage to lose sight of the shore" _Andre Gide

Within the books Ana one of the main characters confesses her feelings to Christian Grey via emails and it got me thinking deeply. I had once used a letter as a way of confessing to my parents that I was smoking which worked wonders and made it far easier. Could I do the same with Mark? Could I finally say all I had wanted to say to my husband but do it under the blanket of an email?

To start with I would send little dirty messages and images that I had found online. I started writing sex scenarios and emailing them to Mark. He would laugh at them and send smiley faces back. I became consumed by sex as I read more and more books of the same genre long after the fifty shades ones were complete. I think Mark for a while got fed up of it all, possibly even felt a little pressured by my constant messages and innuendos so when he didn't reply to my message one day I decided I had to take the opportunity to properly open up to him. I needed to explain to him what was happening to me and why. He needed to know my true feelings and how strong my love was for him.

The email was titled 'Stripped Bare' and underneath it said, "This is not meant as pornography. This is me baring all to you, the man I love". I poured my heart out, told him what the previous year had done to me and how dark a place I had been. I opened up to him about sex, about all what I wanted to explore and that I wanted him to be right there with me as I did so. I was so nervous when I eventually plucked up the courage to press the send button. I sat twiddling my thumbs waiting to see if he would send me a reply. When he did my heart was in my throat and the butterfly's in my stomach were on a frenzy as I opened his mail. He told me that I couldn't off said what I had any better and that he felt exactly the same about me. He even signed off saying "Later's Baby", a saying from my all time favourite book, a book which was saving me and bringing me and Mark closer together than I had ever thought humanly possible.

I bought the audio version of the books so that Mark could listen to them and get a better understanding of where I was coming from. To my excitement he willingly started listening to them in his truck while working. He came home one night with his hands behind his back and whispered in my ear what he wanted to do to me calling me Ana, then proceeding to show me what was behind his back. It was a pile of long black cable ties that he had picked up at work. That's when

I knew he had been listening to the books as Christian buys the cable ties from the hardware store that Ana works at eventually using them on Ana to tie her up. I just couldn't help but smile for all the effort he was making to spice things up between us. Of course he used the cable ties to tie me up and spank me later that night, and I loved it.

Our 8th wedding Anniversary was coming up and thought what better way to celebrate than with a bit of naughty sex. I got a special cheap deal on an executive room in a 4 star hotel in Dundee. I found out that a certain sex toy site had gotten the rights to sell the official Fifty shades sex toys and decided to buy some as well as some other stuff and a nice outfit to go with it. I wanted to be tied up so decided to buy what was called a door jam, so that I could be tied to the door with my hands above my head. I had seen a spreader bar also and was intrigued so it too was added to the basket along with some other things we hadn't used before.

We had a great night away which became a night full of firsts for both of us. I was tied to the glass bathroom door wearing a short silk chemise and a pair of black stockings and high heels, my legs spread with the spreader bar. He knelt in front of me and used his tongue to caress my thigh and between my legs making me soaking wet then proceeding to un cuff me and move me into the walk in shower where he fucked me hard under the cascading water, my breasts pushed against the cold wet tiles, all the while adding to the sensations that were making my head spin with lust. I still had my heels and chemise on which was sticking to me with the water showing every inch of my body making me feel the sexiest I had ever felt in my life.

I managed to deep throat him during foreplay for the first time ever and I went out for our evening meal dressed up with a tight dress with heels, stockings and no underwear, Mark fondling me under the table as we ate. He had recently encouraged me to try a peplum dress to show off my curves and when I did he loved it. He would pinch and slap my arse when passing me and I loved the way it made me feel and the compliments he was giving me was rocketing my confidence. It was an anniversary that will never be forgotten, a time in my life when I felt like a blossoming flower, a caterpillar metamorphosing into a beautiful butterfly spreading her wings.

"For I consider brains far superior to money in every way. You may have noticed if one has money without brains , he cannot use it to his advantage, but if one has brains without the money, they will enable him to live comfortably to the ends of his days"   _L Frank Baum

Chapter Twenty Nine

I had been saving as much money as I possibly could without Mark knowing on the run up to Christmas. I wanted to get him an I-pad as he had wanted one for so long but with all our debts, we couldn't afford one. I always wanted to do good things for my family and friends and would always try and get gifts with meaning. I had once commissioned an artist to do a painting of Marks truck and he cried when he saw it, making me in turn feel good about doing something nice for him. Then one year when I knew Mum and Dad had had a rough year and hadn't had a break, I paid for them to go away on holiday to get away from it all. I just loved making the people around me happy at Christmas. I loved to see their reactions to my gifts.

It was late November and Mark had been up late one night browsing online, had made out that he was Christmas shopping. I went to bed early that night with a smile on my face thinking that he was searching for a perfect gift for me. He never shopped online for any other reason unless he needed something for himself. He always left the gift buying up to me as I was good at picking nice presents and always knew how to get a bargain or move our money around, manage it to a point of making things work.

I had grown used to making lists each week of what we had and hadn't in the cupboards, a list of what meals we had for the week then making it possible to make another list of what we needed for when we did the grocery shop. It kept our money issues at bay, stopped us from buying unnecessary items that we didn't need, it helped us through the months as we slowly got back on our feet financially. Only when there was spare money in the bank would we treat ourselves to something nice.

Working from home meant that most of my earnings were cash

transactions which would only ever end up in the bank account if we needed it for bills. Otherwise it would sit in my cash box and nobody knew exactly what I had as I did the book keeping. That's why it was always so easy to buy gifts for Mark without him knowing what I was getting him. I would fill different envelops within the cash box each week with my cash earnings. Some would go toward Christmas and others towards different things that were coming up, Jacks birthday party being one of them.

It was a week or two later and Mark and I had been arguing about money, only ever did when money was tight. He was getting fed up of the bank account always being empty which wasn't solely my fault. If it hadn't been for me arranging everything, making sure the bills were paid and secretly saving some of my own earnings in order to pay Jacks birthday party and everything for Christmas then there would off been no Christmas to be thankful for. Instead there would off been two very upset children on Christmas morning and again on Jacks birthday when the party he had invited all his friends to had to be cancelled.

Then I found out that on that very night that I thought Mark was searching for the perfect gift for me, he was in fact searching and buying a gift for himself. Not just a few pounds but a light board for his truck worth over £100. I was so angry when I found out, again writing him an email to portray the anger and hurt within me. I had grown tired of having to be the responsible one in the relationship. I was feeling like a complete door mat and craved to be treated in the way that I loved to treat others. I wanted to be surprised, to have some spontaneity in my life. It was the beginning of another spout of depression that I was so accustomed to by now.

December 2012 and Mark and I had had our heart to heart about his selfishness at that time of year and he cancelled his order. His appointment had finally come through for his vasectomy and another era was about to begin as the one with babies was about to end. We were now 100% sure that there were to be no more babies in the Sibbit household. We had got used to the idea and were looking forward to spending the rest of our lives as a family of just the four of us.

When he arrived home from his procedure a lot earlier than expected, for a moment I thought that he had bottled it and hadn't got the procedure done. It hadn't taken as long as expected and he was now home to rest for the remainder of the day. It would take several months before he would eventually get the all clear meaning it was finally safe for us to have sex without the fear on falling pregnant again.

I had made up a sexy Santa sack for us both on Christmas eve, had got myself a sexy Santa outfit complete with white stockings, red heels and a Santa hat. Inside my naughty sack contained a load of sex toys, some stuff I wasn't quite sure of but willing to try. There was anal toys, different lubes, nipple clamps, a doggy strap, spanking paddle, a glass dildo and silly little things like boob stress balls and a fore play version of the game connect four. I wrapped them all up individually and after the kids were bedded early for Santa coming, Mrs Clause entered the room with her sack full of goodies for Mr Clause to open. I just loved seeing his surprise as he seen not only me but of each of the gifts as he opened them. I loved spicing things up and loved that he wanted to try new things with me.

It wasn't all fun and light that Christmas holiday as although I had managed to pull the perfect Christmas day off. What I hadn't catered for was the two weeks that Marks work closed down and the lack of money we both would have over the shut down. I had a small stash of cash put away to pay for Jacks party at the beginning of January but I refused to use it. I wasn't willing to sacrifice his party for the few luxuries we craved. My little boy hadn't had a proper party other than the few he had had at home and he was wanting a party at Pleasureland so that he could invite his class friends. I didn't want to let him down.

We both had almost two whole weeks off for the Christmas holidays and not a single penny to spend on luxury for ourselves. All the bills were to be paid on time but we couldn't even afford to buy ourselves a bottle of vodka to sit and drink while we were relaxing at night in front of the tv.

I became even more depressed the more we had to sit day by

day while we were off with no money to do anything. I wanted to kill myself, started hiding in the bathroom again, crying, willing my life away. The only thing that stopped me was the look on my little boys face when he was celebrating his birthday with all his friends around him. That's when both Shannon and Jack were told that that would be the last of the big parties. Shannon had had a big party where we booked a hall and now Jack had had his. In the years to come they would only be allowed sleepovers and tea parties.

"Home is somewhere that holds those precious memories, when a song or smell brings you right back, a place where you did not live but grew up knowing oh so well, where you felt young and carefree, your sanctuary."

Chapter Thirty

Now that the holidays were over, Jacks party had been and gone and we were both back working full time, we could start looking to the year ahead. We needed a break from it all so decided to start saving to take a trip up north to Kinlochleven. It had been almost 5 years since our last trip and both Shannon and Jack had been too young to remember it. I hadn't really spoken much to my Aunt and Uncle since my Aunty's drunken suicide phone call but I was looking forward to seeing them and to sharing my childhood sanctuary with my own children, most of all I desperately needed to get away from everything. I was still feeling quite glum and needed something to focus my mind on. I needed something to look forward to.

The hotel was booked and family knew that we were coming up to visit so my cousin Holly made arrangements to have the weekend off so to be able to spend some time with us. Holly and I had started to get close over the last few years. Our cousin Charley had got married the year before and Holly and her boyfriend Tim had come down for the event. I was Charley's only bridesmaid and felt honoured. I arranged the hen party of which Holly travelled down for. The three of us as cousins were now closer than we had been as youngsters and it was nice to have that.

"When health is absent, wisdom cannot reveal itself, art cannot manifest, strength cannot fight, wealth becomes useless, and intelligence cannot be applied." _Herophilus

The bond stemmed from that very night at Charley's Hen party. Holly had made the effort to travel down for the night and I was keen for her to meet our friends. It was a great laugh and everyone was really welcoming to Holly who was a stranger to most of the girls there that night. That was apart from Nancy who I later found out to have been a bit stuck up and had left Holly wondering why I could be best friends with such a horrible person. I was completely oblivious to what was going on and completely blinded by her as my best friend.

The wedding was a low key affair as there had been a bit of a divide in the family on the run up to the big day. I wore my red dress that I had worn to my 30th birthday party and walked down the aisle feeling so nervous. I had never been a bridesmaid before and I hadn't liked the feeling of everyone looking at me during my own wedding. I didn't like to feel like people were judging me on how I looked. I didn't feel comfortable within myself at the time and I had known that I needed to lose some weight but hadn't yet felt motivated enough to do so.

We got our pictures taken outside the registrar's which looking back at now I cringe at the sight of. It's a shame really as the happy couple look so happy and I just felt awkward as I was feeling so bad about myself and clearly needed to lose some weight. It was the kick in the butt that I needed to start looking after myself. I had to put myself first for a change. I had to start working out but dreaded the idea of joining a gym so instead I started using my wii fit and cut down on the junk food slowly starting to see a difference in my face. The double chin had to go.

The meal was lovely, an Italian meal at a restaurant just down the road followed by some drinks back at the happy couple's house. Nancy had been invited to join us back at the house and had made a nasty remark about Tim, my cousin Holly's boyfriend not long after they had met for the first time. He had a thistle for a button hole but with him being English she had thought it funny to have a dig at him for wearing one when he wasn't Scottish. I hadn't heard the remark but Nancy had a horrible habit at making nasty remarks about people. She would do so in a jokingly way to try and make herself look funny then turn her back on the person and make a face of disgust. At the time I just didn't see that side of her, was so desperate to have a best friend that I blanked out all the darkness within her.

The wedding cake was a gift from me and Mark which we all had as the dessert back at the restaurant. I was slightly nervous about being served it at the time as I had made it and hated the thought of someone saying that there was something wrong with it. I always doubted myself about any ability I had but at the same time I was proud of myself as I hadn't had much practice with wedding cakes. They had both trusted me to make the image that they had in their heads of what they wanted and seemed to be very happy with the outcome.

"Worry does not empty tomorrow of its sorrow, it empties today of its strength" _Corrie ten Boom

Just days before we were due to go up north to Kinlochleven to visit family I received a phone call shortly after the kids left for school. 'Babes', my pet name for Mark flashed on the screen as I picked up my mobile. It was unusual for him to phone so early in the morning. I had just started getting organised for my own work, was just finishing off some breakfast dishes in the kitchen sink. At first I couldn't make him out. Then in a low shivering voice he told me that the tipper motor had gone over. I asked what he meant to be told that the whole lorry had toppled over onto its side with him in it. Alarm bells started ringing, images in my head of him trapped inside the motor and I can hear the tears filling up in his voice.

I was in shock but still managed to rattle off 100 questions at him over whelming myself. The lorry had gone over onto the passenger side and took him and everything in the truck with it. He had managed to climb up and out of the driver side window having to climb down the underside of the truck. He had just thrown himself onto a pile of stones when he realised his phone was still inside, having to climb back in to find it, his first instinct being to phone his wife. He was on a country road with no help around as the workmen hadn't started their shift yet. He hadn't yet phoned anyone for help or contacted his boss. He was in a state of shock and I couldn't do anything for him. I told him to hang up and contact his work to get help for him after first making sure that he wasn't physically hurt.

Hours had passed and I still hadn't heard back from him. I phoned and phoned but he wouldn't answer until eventually the phone would just go dead when I tried. What was happening and was he ok? All sorts of things were going on in my head. I was frantic with worry.

" Nervous, vomit rising in my stomach, head in a spin. Pacing the floor, around and around in circles. Still no word. Hands shaking, scenes going over and over in my head. Snapping at the kids, jumping every time the phone goes. Looking outside every time a car passes the window. Angry, weepy, should be home by now. 10hrs since 1st phone call. Want to sleep, want to eat, can't do any of it. Can't concentrate, head pounding. Don't want to break when he is walking in the door. Everyone checking in to see if there's any word but .....nothing, he's silent!!!! "

I wrote this down in my note book while I was waiting countless hours to hear if he was ok and coming home. I had never in my life felt so close to the edge. I just couldn't let myself believe that he might not come home. What if he really had been injured and hadn't let on or hadn't noticed with being in shock? Had he managed to get help? I just didn't know. His Dad did all he could to try and find out what was going on but it wasn't until around 8pm that night before he walked through the front door that we all finally knew what had happened. He had had the day from hell, his boss was in no hurry to get help to him, it had been the boys that eventually turned up for shift at the site where he went over that had forced, and taken him to the hospital to get checked over. Apart from being bruised and in shock he was physically ok. It had been several hours later before someone from his work came down to where he was to access the situation, walking right past him to access the truck damage before accessing how Mark was. They hadn't even contacted me about the accident which they should off done with me being the next of kin. If it hadn't been for Mark phoning me himself I wouldn't off known anything about the accident until he came walking in the front door.

It was the final nail in the coffin, confirming that the company had indeed gotten too big and cared more about their image than the people they had working for them. It was the beginning of a long period for Mark where he wanted desperately to get away from a job that he no longer cared for. He was battered and bruised which would heal within days but the emotional scaring inside would take time to heal, was only visible to the people closest to him.

We weren't sure if we would make it up to Kinlochleven as Mark was still really sore but getting away was not only part of a healing process for myself but now Mark needed it too more than anything. On the drive up there I had butterflies in my stomach, I felt nervous about seeing everyone but at the same time I felt like I was going home for the first time in years. We stopped off at the garage where my Uncle and cousin Mick worked in hope of seeing them that day with them both unable to get time off work. Mick was there and for the first time in years he grabbed me and hugged me so tight, almost as if he knew how much I needed it. I had always had a soft spot for him. He was like the big brother that

I didn't have. Driving down the road from the garage at Ballachulish into Kinlochleven, window rolled down, watching the loch follow us all the way to the village, the small houses in the distance growing ever more clearer, I took a deep breath taking in the crisp fresh highland air and knew I was finally there, it was the smell of home and of peace.

"Happiness, true happiness, is an inner quality. It is a state of mind. If your mind is at peace, you are happy. If your mind is at peace but you have nothing else, you can be happy. If you have everything the world can give – pleasure, possessions, power – but lack of peace of mind, you can never be happy" _Dada Vaswani

Over the days that followed I visited my old house in Fort William, showed the kids my old Primary school and stood blissfully watching them as they played in the same spots as I did as a child. I was so happy and didn't want it all to end. Aunt Ivy made us all a Sunday roast and my cousin Danielle invited the kids along to her son Kaden's birthday party. It was so nice to be speaking to everyone again. All our disputes from so many years ago were now long forgotten. We went out for walks, exploring in the trees with the kids, they played by the water tossing stones in the same river we all did as a child and we walked up high into the mountain to get a better view of the village below. I could see the kids eyes light up while we were there, they loved it and I loved to see it. Mark and I both felt like a huge weight had been lifted off our shoulders and we didn't want to go home, even joked about moving there. At that moment in time should he of been offered a driving job up there we would of moved in a flash.

It had been years since I had visited my Gran and Grampas grave, couldn't come home without making a visit to tell them how much they were missed. I didn't want to alarm Mark and the kids by talking out load to a slab of concrete so instead while Mark tidied up the grave and placed the fresh flowers I spoke to them both in my head. I just knew they would hear me, could feel them with me from the moment we got into the car to travel up there. It had been forecast to be a miserable weekend but instead the sun beamed down on us the whole time, like a hot summer day.

"The real voyage of discovery consists not in seeking new landscapes, but in having new eyes" _Marcel Proust

As the lighter nights started to come in both Mark and I were now back at work trying to keep busy. He had started to look for another job but I wasn't very happy about the prospect of him being away from home all the time. For the time being looking for another job was enough to get him through his working days. Mean while I was starting to come back out of my depression. There was a light at the end of the tunnel. Mark and I were at a point in our relationship where I hadn't felt better.

Money wasn't as big a problem as it had been and I was feeling loved. I had fallen in love with the genre of books I was reading and wanted to start writing. The 'Crossfire series' by Sylvia Day were another favourite of mine and the next books to get on audio for Mark to listen too. However it was a book by Nikki Gemmell, 'With my body' that got me into my own writing. A combination of its content and my recent trip up north was enough to inspire me.

I started saving different quotes that I liked online and added them to a book where I added some of my own material. Then I started looking back at my own sexual experiences setting off a light bulb in my head.

I was going to write a book. At first it was going to be about my sexual encounters but the more and more I recollected my experiences and seen the links from one instance to another the more I realised that I needed to put a bit of back ground history to it. I was going to re-live my life and write about it in the truest form I could, from my heart.

I purposely made room in my work diary to have time to write and I loved the relaxing feeling it was producing. I would put on my new Fifty shades of Grey cd and start to look back on my life and piece together why I was the way I was. It brought back memories good and bad and opened my eyes to a deeper version of myself.

I fell in love with classical music because of my new sound track and the relaxed state I would be in when it was on. Mark and I even made love to it one night making it way different to any love making we had ever had before. I started wanting to paint again, looked out all my old art work from college, took pictures of most of it and shared it on my Facebook page where lots of people commented on it making me feel better about myself and my ability as an artist. I bought myself some paint, brushes and a water colour pad and started painting and sketching things again. I re opened a world that had been closed for so long. I was finding more and more ways of expressing my feelings and it was helping me with all the demons I had held inside for so long.

"Life can only be understood backwards: but it must be lived forwards" _Soren Kierkegaard

Nancy had fallen pregnant and at first she felt a bit strange about it around me but I was feeling so much better inside and now I was going to get to be an Aunt. All of us Wow girls were going to be

Aunties. It was actually pretty funny as I remember sitting in my living room with Nancy and Megan, my friend from school who was also friends now with Nancy, we had had coffee a few times and enjoyed the odd catch up. I remember Nancy saying she had this horrible metallic taste in her mouth and Megan and I joked that she was pregnant which later proved to be true. The funny thing was that I also had the same metallic taste in my mouth and throughout her pregnancy I continued to get her pregnancy symptoms almost like we were somehow linked to one another. I wanted to do something special for Nancy so we decided to group together to throw her a baby shower. By now we all knew that Nancy was going to have a little girl and she needed cheering up as she had recently found out her Dad had terminal cancer and she had become his carer. We all chipped in and bought loads of lovely gifts and I wrapped them all up in pretty cellophane with pink bows. I made her a nappy cake which was made out of nappies and baby toiletries and of course it wouldn't be a party without a baby shower cake. I made a baby bump cake complete with an edible picture of her scan photo and some cupcakes with 3d babies on top. The girls helped to prepare the food and decorate my house.

We pretended that we were having one of our girly nights in had everyone arrive earlier than her. She walked into my living room and slowly one by one started noticing everyone, her mum all the way from Newcastle, her sister and friends that wouldn't usually be at one of our girlie nights in. Then she noticed all the decorations and the pile of gifts all for her. She was over whelmed and delighted at the same time. I felt great doing something so lovely for my best friend. Our friendship was now on a better level and she had asked me to be the stand in as birthing partner should her man Arthur not be home from the oil rigs and I couldn't wait to see her little one Amellie. She had chosen a name but only a few of us knew what she was going to be named.

"If you are alone, I'll be your shadow. If you want to cry, I'll be your shoulder. If you want a hug, I'll be your pillow. If you need to be happy, I'll be your smile...but anytime you need a friend, I'll just be me."

It wasn't long after that we all got the bad news that her dad had died. I really felt for her, spent all the spare time I had to be by her side making sure she was ok. On the day of the funeral I met with her and the family beforehand and had a drink with them before heading to the service. At the grave side I stood and watched as she got out of the funeral car, I held our mutual friend Megan's hand as we had arrived together as I knew she was still suffering having had lost her own dad to cancer. I took one look at Nancy as she arrived at the graveside and knew she was going to drop, hurried over to her to hug her tight then passed her over to the capable hands of her man. I stayed late into the night at the wake, she didn't want me to leave her and did all I could to keep her busy in the weeks to come. It had been only weeks before little Amellie was born and soon she had more than enough to keep her busy. I backed off slightly to allow her to have the family time that she needed with her new baby girl.

"I trust him completely – know that I can let go and be totally safe in his care – I can surrender everything over to him – mind, body, soul, senses – He's there with me – I'm his."

Our sex life was back on a high now that my emotional state was healing. We were beginning to get more and more experimental in the bedroom and sex became almost like a hypnotic state of being. I was beginning to completely let myself go. I was unveiling a side of me that I didn't know existed. I felt like a woman with a sexual purpose.

I was working out more when I could and trying to be healthy. In the bedroom I felt like a goddess, I was beginning to love my body for what it was and felt sexy with it. I felt confident and could take naughty pictures of my body and send them to Mark. I even practised lap dancing when on my own in hope that one day I would feel confident enough to do a full one for Mark.

My love for Fifty shades of grey had flourished and I started to follow pages on Facebook with relation to the books. The pages would share everything from bondage to quotes from the books to images of people that could possibly play the characters in the movie which was now rumoured to be getting made. It was while browsing one of these sites that I first laid eyes on the man that had been the perfect image in my head while reading my books. He was my perfect Mr Grey.

Matt Bomer was his name and he was well known in America for his leading role in the hit series 'White Collar'. Luckily for me the show was currently being shown on satellite television and soon I was hooked. Mark would watch it with me and I would tease him, him knowing full well that I saw him as my Christian Grey. That's what was great about our relationship. There was never any jealousy between us. I had the men I would ogle and he would have his women. I would link into his arm and lean my head against his shoulder and tell him that really he was my very own Christian Grey, but he needed to get himself a suit and dress up for me.

I started looking at men in a way that I hadn't before, their features, their stance, the way they walked and how they carried themselves, their ability to make someone laugh and how they would act in a crowd, especially my husband. I was seeing my husband with fresh eyes, almost as if I was seeing him clearly for the first time. I was falling in love with him all over again.

I had never been the sort of woman that liked a man in a suit, always liked a man that looked rugged, like a grafter. But now I was falling in love with the site of a man in a well tailored suit. I realised that men didn't have to be clean shaven to wear a suit. A nice jaw line with stubble, nice eyes and messed up hair with a well tailored suit was a site for sore eyes, made my knees buckle.

I had only once in my life had an orgasm during sex and it had been with Mark the previous year while we were away for our anniversary. I had almost peeked a few times but just couldn't get there but I wasn't really bothered, I had never known sex to be any other way. But now that I was more confident with my body I was beginning to find myself telling Mark what I wanted and where I wanted it leading to the most amazing orgasms I had ever had. Now that he finally knew exactly what I liked he started to do it all the time. He loved to hear, see and taste me as I climaxed always making sure that I did so before him. I would touch myself in front of him and he loved to watch me and feel it as I did so straddling him. My barriers had finally fallen and did so with my husband. I could finally let myself go and get wrapped up in the intimacy.

I had always wanted to have sex in a car and Mark knew this as I had shared my fantasies with him on many occasions knowing that some of them we could bring to life together. It was a Saturday night and the kids were staying at their Grannies to give us a night to ourselves and we decided we were going to fulfil my car fantasy. I put my jacket on with only sexy underwear and stockings underneath and put a pair of black high heels on.

In the car on the way to a nearby beach, I was feeling frisky, couldn't wait so I unzipped his jeans and leaned over to fulfil another fantasy which was to have him in my mouth while he was driving. Seeing him drive always added to my fulfilment when I was in the mood. By the time we arrived he was well and truly ready to have sex. I must say though, as much as it was a thrill, it wasn't half as comfy as it looked in the films. Mark drove home in his boxers that night and had parked the car in the drive then made a run for it into the house before any of the neighbours saw him. What made it all the move funnier was that Skylar had just missed us as I received a text when we were coming home to say she was at our door. A few minutes earlier she would off caught us both wearing very little, knowing fair well what we had been up to.

The girls all knew how frisky 'Fifty shades' had made me, knew I was hooked by it. We would speak openly about sex and they knew that we liked to experiment in the bedroom. Nancy had once said to me "your husband shags you like a porn star and loves you like a princess" and she was right. He was everything I had ever wanted, I was so lucky.

I had badgered Mark for a back massage one night and eventually he gave in. I was lying all relaxed on my stomach on our bed as he massaged some lovely lemon oil into my back gently allowing his thumbs to glide between my cheeks at the base of my spine. I was so relaxed that I hadn't at first noticed when he slipped his finger inside my anus. I was on cloud nine as he circled his finger inside me as his others reached around and rubbed my clit at the same time. I had a very slow building, orgasm, so relaxed that soon he was inside me. We were successfully for the first time having anal sex and I was so relaxed, loving all the feelings it was producing. Before long I was building up to my second climax which got my head in a spin and I raised my butt slightly to allow Mark to start banging into me like he normally would when it was my vagina. He reached around and continued to rub my clit as he grew closer to his own orgasm. It felt so good, grabbing my arse as he banged into me full force finding his own peak. It was a night that started off a whole other form of sexual pleasures for us both. We had finally conquered the taboo of anal sex.

Probably the most intense sex I had ever had been when we decided to use the butt plug for the first time. We were having sex doggy style on our bed when Mark slowly while distracting me by rubbing my clit, stuck the butt plug into my backside. He then placed himself into my vagina and placed the doggy strap around my waist, tilting my pelvis upwards to gain deep penetration. He banged really hard into me until he could wait no longer and whipped out the butt plug replacing it with his penis. We both had very intense orgasms, falling asleep instantly afterwards. My legs were like jelly on awakening, struggling to go to the bathroom, a grin on my face at the thought of how great our sex life had become.

He would spank me during sex and I loved it, loved to see the red marks on my arse cheeks as I walked past the hall mirror on the way to the bathroom afterwards. He started pulling my hair, scraping it back into a pony tail just before his climax. Tugging it with one hand and pinning my arse in place as he banged into me. I loved all of it.

Our anniversary again and we booked into an executive room at the Apex hotel in Dundee. Our room was on the corner of the building with floor to ceiling windows on two walls with views over the river Tay. We had all our toys with us and Mark had got me a nice new sexy number to wear. He positioned me onto the desk in front of one of the window walls and fucked me silly. It was dark outside and we kept the lights inside on so that we could be seen by the people working in the office building across the road. Boy was it a thrill, we were becoming exhibitionists but they didn't know us and we didn't know them so there was no harm. Later we relaxed in the hotel pool and fondled each other in the hot tubs, steam room and sauna.

Looking back now it was so crazy, we were like animals, our libidos on a constant high. It was like we were in our honeymoon phase only we had already been together for almost 13 years. The sex was getting better as we aged.

" When the cracks of friendships begin to show, family unite. A time in our life when we realise who really matters, who never did and who always will. The people who really care for you come forth, for our family are what matters the most. Be our hearts blessed and the blanket of our family exist forever more. "   _Mary L Sibbit

Chapter Thirty One

January 2014 and the start of what is due to be a very busy year. The Christmas holidays were celebrated in a style that we were accustomed too. I commissioned Archie an old friend from college to do a painting of Marks current truck as his gift. I had originally enquired about it just before Marks accident but had to put it on hold until I was 100% sure that Mark was getting his truck back.

I knew that Mark still wanted a new job but up until Christmas he had turned down everything that had come his way. He was confused about what he wanted to do. A job would come up and it was either paying too little or it was situated too far away. I had gotten used to the idea of the possibility of Mark going back on the distance and told him that if it was what he needed to do to be happy then I would support his decision, I would learn to get used to it. I even looked into shortening my hours and started organising the cake business to suit going back to a life where I would have to cope on my own on week days.

We had gotten Jack the Xbox that he wouldn't stop asking for before Christmas and I had gotten Shannon One Direction concert tickets. Skylar had seen them online and asked all the girls if we fancied it, knowing that I desperately wanted them for Shannon after failing to get them the year before. I was the only one at the time who was up for it so we only got the four tickets. Later Nancy decided she wanted them for Katie too so she eventually managed to get her hands on some so we could all go together even though we wouldn't be seated together.

It was going to be Chloe, Skylar's daughter's birthday while we were away so we decided to make a day and night of it, travelling by train and staying overnight. Nancy was being a bit of a pain not making her mind up about what she wanted to do, whether she was staying overnight or not. Then she decided to ask a friend to join us. It meant that we had to wait and see what her plans were, had us hanging on not knowing as to what to book for the travelling and the accommodation. Eventually Skylar and I decided we weren't waiting any longer as all the hotel rooms were getting booked up and we didn't want to miss a good opportunity.

At first I wasn't too impressed about the arrangements. I had wanted my own privacy with my own room with Shannon but it was going to be too much money having left it so late booking. I felt nervous about sharing my privacy with Skylar. Not because of Skylar herself but because of my anxiety and toilet fears. I was a bit worried about it all as I was starting to get the tell tale sights of a flare up of my Ibs and was feeling a bit anxious about not having my own space. Little did I know that that was nothing compared to what was about to hit me.

Back to January 2014 and I was now saving really hard for Mums birthday. It was Mums 50th birthday on the 3rd of February and we had booked a hall to have a party. We were going all out like my 30th, only this time it was a 1950's themed party. One of Mum's favourite movies was Grease and we wanted to have the American 1950's feel.

During the summer in 2013 I had been at a wedding fair with the business and there was a band playing there that Mum loved. They were perfect for the night being a blues band. The Declaration Band we're a lot of money but I promised Mum I would book them for the night and pay for them as part of her gift for her birthday. I had already paid the £100 deposit when I booked them but now I needed the further £300 to pay them on the night.

On the big day I was meant to get my hair done by Nancy but she had let me down and I ended up doing it myself. My cousin Holly and her now fiancé Tim were down for the party and we took them around to Mum and Dad's so they could meet properly first before going to the party. We were all dressed up in our 1950's poodle skirt dresses, Shannon had a Pink ladies outfit on and Jack had a t birds one. Mark got the proper black and white shoes online and wore them with black dress trousers, black shirt, white tie and braces and waist coat and a black and white hat to finish his look. I had made the cake as a surprise to be revealed to Mum when we were up at the hall decorating that afternoon and everyone was taking pictures of it and complimenting me on its awesomeness. I had carved it into a jukebox complete with lights with an Americans diner scene with the Grease logo and a milkshake. Dad and I made the buffet and served it hot and cold throughout the night.

It was a great night filled with memories but I was disappointed with a few of the girls. Nadine had tried her best to avoid me repeatedly asking her for an answer to whether she was coming to the party or not and Tess had said she didn't have the money even though everyone had been informed about the event months in advance. Nancy was my biggest let down as even though she did eventually turn up late, she had let me down with my hair and spent most of the night making daggers at my cousin Holly for no reason. She was being a bitch and I hadn't noticed that in her at first.

Holly and I had desperately tried to get Mum and Aunty Ivy speaking again after having falling out with each other years ago and we had hoped Mum would invite her sister to her party. Unfortunately it didn't happen but we were both hopeful that Mum and Dad wouldn't let Holly down by not attending her and Tim's wedding later that year. I even resorted to emailing Mum about my true feeling about her falling out and how I was sad about her not going up north to visit her parent's grave and being able to share all her memories of her birth place with her grandchildren. I knew I was pulling at heart strings but it was a last resort, the final push to try and build bridges. I knew Mum loved hearing the stories we had told her when we had had our trip up north the previous year and she had helped Shannon with a school project about Kinlochleven. I knew deep down she was thinking about it all, she just needed a push to unravel her stubbornness.

It was at Mum and Dad's house before Mum's party that Holly had asked her if they were going to come to the wedding and Mum said she couldn't miss her big day. At last there was some hope but we still weren't completely convinced. In the weeks that followed Mum started asking about where we were staying and eventually booked a room at the hotel where we were staying and where the wedding was being held. They only booked the one night so they didn't have to hang around but it was a start. They were going to be in the same room as each other for the first time in years and even though I had no idea what way the relationship would end up I was hopeful that all would work itself out.

It was a few weeks after Mum's party and the revelation that they were going to attend Heathers wedding that I had probably the most emotional dream that I had ever had in my life. I always had weird dreams that would contain my Gran on dad's side but on this night for the very first time I found myself dreaming of my Grandpa, Mums Dad. I dreamt that he had come down from heaven for one night only and he was sitting on a bean bag with the whole family around him. I knelt down in front of him and he gave me the warmest biggest hug I had ever felt in my life. I kissed him and told him how much I loved him and he told me how wonderful my children were. He told me not to worry about Shannon but to keep an eye on Jack. I felt loved then in that moment I woke and I felt a sense of loss. I wanted to fall back asleep so I could see him again. I spent most of that day thinking about him and what the dream must off meant. The day we are finally reunited I want to have that same feeling. I want him to greet me with a hug just like the one in my dream.

"When I see you, I never want to look away. When I dream of you, I never want to wake up. When I hug you, I never want to let go. But now I realise I have to."

I was starting to really look after myself again by getting back into an exercise routine. I had been in contact with and old school friend Jake who was now a 'Herbalife' distributer and health coach. I started drinking the healthy milkshakes on the days that I was working out to get all the nutrients that my body wasn't getting from the meals I was having. With the extra support from him and actually enjoying the workouts I was soon loosing not only pounds in weight but inches off in different areas of my body. I started to realise that it was important to not only not skip any meals but I needed to have healthy snacks in between meals to keep my metabolism going. I was a bit sceptical about it at first but it was proving to be right when I started to notice the differences in my body and the way I was feeling. I started to learn about the importance of protein and how it would aid with the weight loss. I also found out about what exercises to do and in what manner to work the areas that I wanted to look better or lose the weight from. I was feeling great.

In March I was meant to be going to my first ever Cake international down in Manchester. It was a big event for everyone who loved cake decorating and I wanted to go to suss it out in hope of competing in one of their competitions one day. Unfortunately just days before we were due to go my Ibs got really bad and I felt unable to travel long distance. We had to cancel the hotel we were booked into and lost not only the deposit we had paid but also the event tickets that I had paid for online. I was gutted that I was feeling that way but I just knew I couldn't force myself to go. It would kick start my anxiety and at the time I wasn't ready to conquer it head on. Ibs 1- me 0 I let it beat me.

All was not lost though as because I had been saving to go I now had the money burning a hole in my purse. We decided to spend the day in Perth which wasn't too far for me to travel. We went to Frankie and Bennies for lunch and did a bit of shopping. Mark decided to finally purchase the suit I had been dying to see him in and boy was he a site for sore eyes. He decided on a dark grey suit complete with waist coat and I couldn't wait for him to wear it while we were alone.

"So sweet and delicious do I become, when I am in bed with a man who I sense, loves and enjoys me, that the pleasure I bring excels all delight, so the knot of love, however tight it seemed before, is tied tighter still." _ *Veronica Franco*

That weekend we had spent some quality time together and the sex was magical. We were both really horny and we fooled around with each other under covers as we chilled out in front of the tv. He whispered in my ear that he wanted to be in my mouth so I dragged him into the kitchen to get on my knees to perform the act, making eye contact with him for the first time ever doing so. It felt exhilarating and naughty as the kids were in the next room still watching tv. Once the kids were in bed we both dressed up, me in sexy underwear, stocking and heels, Mark in his suit and had dirty sex on the living room floor with sex toys. At the time I actually had my period but it never stopped Mark when he wanted to play, he didn't care about the mess and nor did I when I was so horny.

Early Monday morning Mark woke me up still feeling really horny from the night before and caressed my back with his hands and mouth as I awaked lying on my stomach. He entered me from behind, pulled my head up towards him and whispered into my ear that he was going to phone in sick to his work so that we could fuck me like that all day. It made me melt and pushed me closer to my climax. He did exactly that, he phoned in sick and when the kids eventually went to school we both went back to bed and had more sex. We sneaked out for lunch to a local pub so that no body from his work seen him and had a lovely day together just the two of us. It was the following day when he had to stay away with his work that I felt like a love sick teenager. I was so in love with my husband, got butterflies talking to him when he was away from home.

I don't know how many times it's possible to fall in love with another human being but it felt like we were breaking all the boundaries when it came to our love for each other. We never fell out of love but would always find another form of love, a deeper more intense form of it and sex was a major factor in finding such heights.

"A friendship is like a vase, once it gets broken you can't fix it...you may try to glue it but you can't get rid of the cracks that will sooner or later separate again." *_Yushiie Iigmiir*

April and it was little Amellie's 1st birthday. I had made a massive 5 tier cake for her party for a gift, had made another cake also for her cake smash and paid for a photographer to come and take some professional photos. I also bought Amellie her first computer tablet, a vetch baby tablet. I had spent a fortune but was hoping to get some great photos of the cake smash for my portfolio with it being my first one.

When Nancy decided she wanted Amellie to be photographed in just a nappy and tutu I didn't think at first but when the photographer was leaving and Nancy said to her she didn't want the pictures to be up online I was a bit shocked and disappointed. She knew I wanted the pictures for my portfolio and that they would be showcased on my business page. I had paid for it all for absolutely nothing. I felt used and very disappointed in her after everything I had done for her.

Mark had been seeing that side of Nancy for a while but I kept brushing his remarks aside as I couldn't see past my best friend. He wanted me to stop being a mug and see her for what she was and slowly I was coming around to his line of thinking. I was so disappointed that eventually we had words about the whole thing as I couldn't let it lie this time. In the end we sorted it out but the cracks in our friendship had started to show.

The following month it was Holly's hen party up in Inverness. My cousin Charley and I had booked into the same bed and breakfast as the rest of the girls. I paid for our accommodation while Charley paid for the train fair up there. I was feeling a bit nervous about sharing with someone and with travelling. I wasn't a big drinker anymore and I didn't want to be seen as a bore, so I tried to see it as a trial run to see how I would get on as I was going to Edinburgh with Skylar and the girls the following month.

Mark drove us through to Perth where we got a direct train into Inverness. We met all the rest of the girls in the pub at the train station and had our first few drinks. We got changed into out camouflage gear that the chief bridesmaid had gotten for us all and went for lunch in a local bar. Later we checked into the bed and breakfast which was really nice and spacious. I was starting to feel more at ease now that we had arrived and had met everyone who all seemed to be lovely. We all got dressed up and got chauffeured around town in a limousine which was a surprise for Holly.

Then we ate at Jimmi chungs the Chinese buffet but my cousin Danielle and I weren't feeling great after the champagne in the moving limo. A few bars later and Danielle and I decided to go back to the hotel for an earlier night than expected. On route back in the rain I discovered that the two of us weren't all that different. She too had the same stomach and bowel problems as me and it was nice to share things with her. I didn't feel so much as a bore as I wasn't the only one going to bed early. I had travelled up there, spent and good part of the night with everyone and I knew my limits.

The next day we all had breakfast together and said our goodbyes as Charley and I boarded the train and the rest of the girls made their way to the bus station. It was a long tiring journey home but I was glad that I didn't have a hangover. Mark picked us up at Perth and I was so glad to see his face. It had only been one night but I had missed him so much.

It was around this time that Mark got another job offer from the company that had taken over the company he used to work for. He had been offered one just before Christmas but with it being that time of year he didn't feel secure jumping into another job. This was another offer from the same company and he didn't know what he wanted to do. I was starting to get annoyed with him for not making his mind up. One minute he is taking the job then something was said that made him change his mind. I was starting to get stressed out between not knowing if he was going to take a job being away from home and my work was starting to stress me out at the same time with it being so busy. I needed a proper break to reflect and see what I really wanted from the business. I needed it to be a happy work place again before I gave up on it for good.

I tried to speak to Nancy about it, really needed someone to talk to but every time we were together she would have other friends around and I never got a chance to speak to her properly. I was losing my best friend. They all had something I didn't which was a baby and I couldn't compete with them.

The day we left for Edinburgh I was again feeling anxious. I had tried to speak to Nancy about it but she would always say it would be fine just had a drink and chill out. That was her answer to everything. She was very much still a party animal even though she now had three children and was almost 30 years old. I was beginning to feel like I couldn't speak to her like what we used to. She was spending more and more time with other friends that had young children just like her. I was feeling pushed aside.

There had been a little bit of tension between Nancy and Skylar about the arrangements for the travelling and accommodation to Edinburgh. Nancy was always a last minute type of girl where Skylar and I liked to be organised. I was starting to get tired of Nancy's constant moaning about other people and her back stabbing and bitchiness. Mark was seeing it and had seen it for a long time. I was starting to see it now and I didn't like it. It was bringing me down and at times I was feeling unlike myself as she would drag me into conversations that I didn't want to be included in. Almost everyone within our group of friends and out with was getting harsh words said about them and I started to wonder if she could say that about so many close friends then what was she saying about me.

It had been a few weeks previous that she started an argument in a private group message online with Nadine. Nancy and I had previously spoken to each other about how over protecting Nadine was with her two girls so when Nadines daughter got to walk home from school for the first time but ended up popping in at mine to use the toilet instead of going straight home, war broke out. Nancy basically told her to lighten up. I stupidly tried to stick up for Nancy but it ended up backfiring on me and I ended up the bad one. I may off said more than I should off, some home truths that may off sounded harsh but I meant every word, I apologised for the manner that I had said it but I wasn't sorry for what I had said.

For a long time Nadine had been topic of conversation with a lot of people. Everyone felt that she was putting her children second after her job as they were always panned off on the grandparents so that she could do extra shifts at work and spend weekends at the football with her husband Glenn. It was not only us girls that said it but people at her work were bad mouthing her for stealing other people's shifts and acting like she ruled the roost. I was told by one of her co workers that even her parents and Glenn weren't happy with her and I kind of mentioned it in our argument.

I wouldn't reveal who it was that was talking about her which in the end made her even angrier. I should off just kept my mouth shut but it was what it was. Looking back I was being more influenced by Nancy than I cared to admit. I would never off been so harsh with someone if I was my normal self, but Nadine had hurt me a few times in the past and deep down I didn't trust her. She had been the person that went around telling everyone about my miscarriages as if it was just a piece of gossip for her. I had never forgiven her for it. For weeks she ignored all Nancy and my messages but eventually she started coming out for breakfast again with us all.

On the train journey to Edinburgh I was glad to be sitting with Skylar and our two girls. Skylar was a lot more sympathetic towards me and my toilet issues and I felt at ease sitting with her. Nancy was on the same train but in another carriage but once we were moving she joined us in seats across the aisle from us as they were empty. It was a good laugh but it wasn't like it should off been. On the train we discovered that the hotel Nancy was staying at wasn't the same one as ours. I wasn't too bothered as I was feeling more at ease with Skylar and didn't really want to be too close to Nancy. Skylar and I both understood that this trip away was for the girls and the concert but Nancy just wanted to have a drink and have fun. I had no interest what so ever in having a drink.

We checked into our hotel and chilled out for a bit after we had had lunch together as a group. It was a time for me, Skylar and our girls to bond and have a laugh. It was Chloe's birthday the next day so we did a bit a investigating into what we would do the next day before we got the train home.

The Concert was brilliant, it had been the biggest concert in Scottish history and we had been a part of it. We all had a ball and thankfully Nancy and Katie were sitting in a different area from where we were.

We had left them just inside the gates then met them afterwards to catch the tram back to Princess Street to make our way separately back to our hotels. After the girls had fallen asleep Skylar and I put up banners and balloons in the hotel room so that Chloe would get a surprise when she woke. We had breakfast in bed then made our way back to Princess Street to meet Nancy and Katie. We decided to go to Pizza hut for lunch then went to a cool illusionist place just outside Edinburgh castle. We were all knackered on the train ride home but it had been a success. I hadn't had any panic attacks while away I had really enjoyed myself.

A couple of weeks later we were going up north for Holly and Tim's wedding and Nancy had promised to colour and cut my hair. I had been at her for months to do my hair and she said she would but pinning her down to actually do it was like trying to get blood from a stone.

She had always been fairly unreliable but by now it was ridiculous. As it got closer to the wedding and knowing I desperately needed it done for then she promised to do it for me so I took her for her word.

On the day it was meant to get done she texted to apologise and to say she didn't have the colours she needed so to make up for it she had booked me into a hair salon to get it done professionally. I was actually shocked as she was actually doing something for me for a change. But really, it hadn't quite been what she promised, she had just chucked her partners money at the situation, panned me off, yet another moment when she couldn't give up her precious time for a friend. She had known about it for weeks and still didn't bother her arse to get the products even after me reminding her.

I wasn't feeling very well that day, had been back and forth to the toilet so wasn't feeling too sure about leaving the house to go get my hair done. She had at least made some sort of effort to book me in and pay for it so I couldn't let her down by refusing to go. I made it down there but the whole 5 hours that I was in there I thought I was going to either be sick or have to use their bathroom. At first I just thought it was my anxiety but when it didn't where off I began to think it must actually be a tummy bug. Usually my anxiety when going somewhere would ease off as soon as I got there but this time it hadn't and I was exhausted by the time I eventually got home.

Nancy had always known about the money shortages that Mark and I had suffered so when she offered to lend me some to go up north for the wedding I took it as a sign that she did care. The money wasn't actually hers but her partner Arthur's. She said it was ok after everything I had done for them all in the past. Did she still actually care about our friendship or was she just chucking money at her problems again? I now believe it was the latter.

I didn't really want her money, felt really guilty taking it but she insisted. We had the money we needed to go up but I wasn't sure if it was enough to actually enjoy ourselves without worrying. I didn't tell

Mark about it as I knew how he felt about her. I just tucked it into the bottom of my handbag for emergency use only. I wish now I hadn't accepted it as we didn't even need it and soon after arriving home I gave the whole lot back with my gratitude to her for the short lend.

"Anxiety is loves greatest killer. It makes others feel as you might when a drowning man holds onto you. You want to save him, but you know he will strangle you in his panic"   _Anais Nin

Chapter Thirty Two

Our weekend up north for Holly and Tims wedding was a pleasant one, filled with happiness and reunions. Mum and Dad made it up for the big day and although I could tell they were nervous it went well. I was nervous for them, had been feeling a bit anxious the whole time, not knowing if they would all actually make up and become a happy family again after all of Holly and I's efforts to bring the family back together. I had tears in my eyes when My Aunt and Uncle approached Mum and Dad on the patio and hugged them both, joking about how long it had been.

I had been feeling a little off since the day I had got my hair done but the travel up wasn't near as bad as it could off been. We settled in to the hotel and I arranged for the cake to be stored safely so it didn't get damaged. I had designed a 5 tier wedding cake as a surprise gift for the happy couple. They knew they were getting it but had no idea of what it would look like. I also did a painting for them to match the cake and their chosen theme and got it framed. I was getting my confidence back being an artist and I wanted to do something a bit different for them. I was just glad to get the cake unloaded from the car, had always been anxious when delivering a cake and this had been the longest cake journey yet. I needed to assemble it and finish it off the following day before all the guests arrived but for a while I could now relax.

That night we met some of the other guests as they too arrived and checked in for the weekend. We all chipped in and stayed up late decorating the hotel for the next day. I hadn't managed to eat anything other than toast and a bit of a sausage roll that day and was feeling a bit weak. I just wanted the sick bug or whatever it was to disappear. I had taken all the medication I could and went to bed in hope that the next day would be a better one.

About half an hour before the ceremony, Mum, Dad and my brother Dylan all arrived and checked in just as I was finishing off curling my hair. It was a mad rush for them all to get ready. I was nervous and still feeling a bit off. I had been sick early in the morning and still wasn't sure if it was a bug or if it was just my anxiety that was making me so ill.

The ceremony was beautiful. My Uncle walked Holly across the grass with a piper leading the way. It was funny as his kilt was too long and a small joke was made about him cutting the grass. There was always a bit of comedy involved when my Uncle was about. It was what made him such a lovable person. Mark and I had stopped off in Broughty Ferry on the way up to pick up both my cousin Mick and Uncle's kilts, unfortunately at the time we also gained a parking ticket for our efforts. They wanted the Rangers tartan and could only get it from the shop we had to collect it from in Broughty Ferry.

We all sat on the patio and happily watched the happy couple say their vows followed by photos which was when Mum, Dad, my Uncle and Aunt all made peace with each other. After the photos the kids got to take part in a scramble each gaining a big heap of money. Jack filled his sporran and Shannon her handbag. We had gotten Jack fitted for a kilt and hired one, picking it up with the others, that way he could be like his dad wearing the Royal Stewart tartan.

The meal was lovely but I struggled to eat much of it. My appetite just wasn't there anymore and I was finding myself having to force feed myself. Holly and Tim were over the moon with the cake and had tears in their eyes as they hugged me and thanked me. Tim even started crying during his speech as he thanked me for it, getting side tracked and forgetting to thank others for different things. He later stood up to thank them apologising for forgetting them in the original speech. I was presented with a present bag from them both containing some lovely gifts as a big thank you for everything I had done for them. I just wasn't expecting anything from them as it was what I did. I liked to do nice things for others, never expecting anything in return.

I went up to bed early that night, didn't stay up late with everyone else as I was feeling rotten. The next day we all met for breakfast and again I was finding that I needed to force feed myself. We went for a nice walk down towards the loch for some fresh air. Our hotel room looked onto the loch with its stunning views and I just didn't want to go home. We were staying another night but Mum, Dad and Dylan were leaving that day. We had all arranged to go into Kinlochleven to see my Aunt and Uncle. We led the way and stopped off at the graves so that Mum could visit her parents.

It was nice all sitting having a laugh together like the old times. We went for a walk around the village to show Mum and Dad all that had changed and Kaden, Danielle's son that Mum and Dad had met for the first time at the wedding came with us to play with Shannon and jack. When they left Mum and Aunty Ivy hugged each other tight and promised to keep in touch, and it was like this weight lifting off my shoulders, so warm and comforting to see them at long last speaking again. All my hopes and prayers had been answered.

Later that day all the guests who were staying at the hotel for the whole weekend like ourselves all met up in Fort William to have a family meal, which Holly and Tim kindly paid for. It was so nice to all be together, was just a shame that Mum and Dad weren't there. It was a sort of last supper as a lot of Tim's family had a long journey back down into England. I met so many lovely people that weekend.

The next morning we were all packed to come home too and I was still feeling like crap. I was sitting in my Aunt's living room and started to feel the onset of a panic attack. I had been running back and forth to the toilet and my tablets still hadn't kicked in. I had to go outside for fresh air and take deep breathes to work through it. I still hadn't managed to eat a full meal and I was feeling awful. We said our goodbyes and slowly made our way home, stopping off whenever I needed a break. It could off been way worse as eventually the tablets kicked in stopping me going to the toilet leaving just the nausea to deal with.

"Never ignore a person who loves and cares for you. One day you may realise you've lost the moon while counting the stars."

In the morning before we left to come home Nancy had phoned me to see how the wedding was not realising that we still hadn't left to come home. As I was feeling like crap, I told her truthfully how I was feeling and tried to speak to her about my anxiety only to have the phone call cut short by her, which at the time thought it was a bit odd.

A few weeks later and Nancy still hadn't made an effort to see me. I had messaged her a few times to catch up but she always had an excuse. I was feeling absolutely rotten as I still wasn't eating properly. I had been to the doctors and they had said it must be some kind of virus. Not once had I had any sort of virus that lasted this long so I wasn't completely convinced.

A local young girl had had an accident while on holiday with her dad and Nancy had decided to take upon herself to raise funds to get her mum on a plane to be there to be with her very poorly daughter. I thought it was great what she was doing and did only what I could while being ill by giving her not only a donation of money but loads of kids items to sell at a car boot and a voucher from the business to raffle off at one of her events.

She would go on about how much help the family needed and how close she was with them but it had actually been the first time in the many years that Nancy and I had known each other that she had even mentioned them. I thought it was a bit odd at the time but it was a great thing that she was doing for the family. She had this habit of feeling or acting like she was close with everyone and anyone, names would pop up in conversation out of nowhere, people she had never spoken about in front of us before but all of a sudden they were the best of friends. Sometimes people she had been friends with she was suddenly very nasty about one minute then the next she couldn't do enough for them and that got me very weary of her.

While she was being consumed with the fundraising I was laid up at home feeling rotten. I didn't go out much as I didn't have the energy. I started having palpitations and still couldn't eat. I couldn't exercise with being so ill but still the weight was starting to fall off me. The doctor then decided that it must be my Ibs and not a bug that was causing my ill health and changed my medication which to start with seemed to help a little. He referred me to get both a sigmoidoscopy and an endoscopy to examine down my throat into my stomach and up into my bowels but it would take time for the appointment to come through.

Only days after seeing the doctor I started getting really bad pains in my lower right side and I was sent straight through to Ninewells with suspected appendicitis. While this was happening I was messaging the girls to let them know and Nancy was being quite dry and bitchy with me. Ah you'll be fine etc, etc. I had had almost enough as I could with her being so unsupportive. Fair enough it turned out not to be appendicitis but an inflamed bowel but she didn't know the outcome of my hospital visit as she never even once asked after I was discharged.

She had turned up at my door one morning with little Amellie wanting to use my laptop to set up a charity page for the young girl she was fundraising for. I was sitting on the couch watching tv feeling absolutely rotten when she turned around to me and told me she would give me Amellie for the day and it would sort me out. She honestly thought I was moping around at home feeling sorry for myself. I just wanted her out, tried to explain to her how ill I actually was only for her to turn her back on me and make out there was nothing wrong with me. She left shortly afterwards when I had nothing else to say to her. It was the first time I had ever felt so much hatred toward her and the first time she wasn't welcome in my home.

A charity psychic night had been organised with proceeds going towards the cause that Nancy was raising money for and I had said to her before her visit that day that I would go with her. After our wee argument

I really didn't want to go and at first told her that I couldn't make it, just made up an excuse but it was actually Mark who encouraged me to go as I needed to get out and about and he wanted to see me to enjoy myself.

I then thought it would be the perfect opportunity to try and make amends with Nancy, a chance for us to bond again seeing that it was something that we were both interested in. Unfortunately it didn't go as planned. To start with her man Arthur was there and when we arrived I found that we weren't actually having an one on one girly night out but a load of her other friends were there also.

From the off I felt uncomfortable, felt so unwelcome. I had this over whelming feeling in my gut that something wasn't right and because I wasn't drinking I felt like an outcast. Nancy made no effort what so ever to make me feel welcome so I made my excuses and left early. There was a dark storm brewing and little did I know that the heavens were about to burst open.

The following Sunday was a fundraising day that Nancy had organised and she had asked to borrow my gazebo. When she didn't turn up for it after me hunting all the bits out of the shed I was pretty pissed off. I had told her that I wouldn't be at the event as my Dad was coming over to help Mark fit my new kitchen work tops and secretly I didn't want to go as I would of felt like an outcast by her and all her new friends.

On the morning she texted me to see if I was coming up but I ignored it as I was so mad with her. Instead I sat out in the back garden with my Mum and the kids and had a lovely day in the sun. We did the lunch rounds collecting it from a local bakery with my kitchen being all disconnected, bumping into Megan while out who questioned why I wasn't at the event. I just told her the same that I told Nancy. I was busy with my kitchen refit.

The following day I was added to a group message that Nancy had made on Facebook about her up and coming 30th birthday. I made the effort to tell her that I would be there with bells on even though deep down I didn't want to be. She completely ignored my response while responding to everyone else which pissed me off even more.

With it being a group message with about 30ish people in it, my phone was constantly beeping every time someone responded. I was trying to work and was feeling really crappy so I left the conversation not thinking anything of it. A few hours later a got a nasty message from Nancy asking what the hell was wrong with me? Why was I not taking any interest in her and why didn't I come to support her at the fundraising day? That was it, I snapped, the thunder clouds brewing up inside me burst with anger.

I told her exactly why I was the way I was, told her I was sick of her selfishness and her lack of interest in my life. Everything had to be her way all the time, everyone else's lives had to revolve around her and I was sick of it. She told me there was nothing wrong with me and that I was just feeling sorry for myself. That's when I told her if she had been any type of friend that she would off saw it differently. I had been there for her with so many things. I had been there though her dad's death, her health issues, her rocky relationship with her partner, her pregnancy, the list was endless. I felt it wasn't too selfish of me to ask her in return for a little bit of support.

Then she lashed out by telling me that she and the other girls had all been talking about me behind my back and that I was pathetic. I had nearly not made it to Shannon and Jacks sports day as I was being sick all morning. Luckily it got postponed in the morning but because I hadn't gone out for breakfast instead with the girls that morning I was the bad one. I knew that afternoon when I arrived at the sports day that something was up. Nancy hadn't come as she had to go view a new house but Nadine and Tess were both quite dry with me. I knew at the time that they had been talking about me, I could sense it, almost like when walking into a busy room that suddenly goes silent. So when Nancy confirmed it in our argument I knew she was telling the truth. I was so angry when she said I had nothing wrong with me that in retaliation I told her a few home truths of my own. She was a hypochondriac, that in fact it was her that always had something bigger or worse wrong with her, if anyone had something wrong with them her issue was always worse or more important and I was sick of hearing her crap. Her response was that it was all because her dad had died the year previous and how dare I bring it up. I hadn't brought it up. I had simply told her I was sick of her constant moaning and bitching about everyone and everything. I told her not to dare bring her dads death into it as it had nothing to do with our argument and I wasn't having her bad mouth me about something I hadn't said.

I never spoke to her again that day but as soon as Nadine heard we had had words she texted me out of the blue wanting to know what happened. She never texted me so I knew she was just wanting a piece of gossip so gave her as little info as possible but made sure she knew that Nancy and I would not be speaking again.

"Don't worry about what people say behind your back, they are the people who are finding faults in your life instead of fixing faults in their own life."

In the days that followed I felt useless, I knew everyone was talking about me and getting Nancy's side or the argument. I didn't see why I needed to justify myself to anyone as I wasn't depressed and feeling sorry for myself like she was making out. I actually was ill and had all the medications to prove it. Had she been around like she should of been having supposed to have been my best friend then she would of seen that it was the truth.

She carried on sending nasty text messages to me and it was starting to stress me out, making me feel worse than I already was. She said that I had been posting nasty stuff about her online which I hadn't, again having to justify myself to her. I explained that whoever was telling her these things needed to stop trying to make the situation worse. I blocked her from my page and eventually had to block her number on my mobile after an afternoon when she started continuously sending me nasty texts. She threatened me, told me that I wouldn't be so cocky if she turned up at my door. I hadn't done anything wrong. She had been listening to people who were making up stories. That same afternoon Mark had come home early and I completely broke down in front of him, I couldn't take anymore of the stress. I had told her to move on and get on with her life and to let me get on with mine but she wouldn't leave me alone. She lived for the drama.

A couple of weeks later I was up visiting Skylar, seeing her new home as she had recently moved but I wasn't sure if she knew about me and Nancy falling out. She hadn't mentioned it and had so much to tell me so I just left it at first. Once she was done telling her stories I decided I would ask her if she knew. I was actually surprised to learn that she didn't. The gossip merchants hadn't reached her. I explained to her my side of the story and she was quiet as she listened to every word. When I was finished she apologised to me as she admitted that yeah in fact that morning of the kids sports day, at breakfast they had all been talking about me and Nancy was making out to everyone that I was just depressed and Skylar admitted saying that I needed a kick up the back side, actually not realising that I was ill. That's when I opened up to her about everything that I couldn't with Nancy. She was really understanding but still hopeful that one day Nancy and I would make up. I explained to her how upset and let down by Nancy I was and that I could never trust her again with anything, not after all that she had done and said about me behind my back.

I didn't like the fact that I had to justify myself to people about my illness being something physical and not mental. After all depression was an actual illness of which millions of people suffer so really did it matter what was wrong with me? It was the lack of the support from the people that were meant to be my close friends that was my problem. The real issue for Nancy was that all eyes weren't on her if someone else had a problem, not that I was feeling sorry for myself, which I wasn't. I realise that now after months of going over and over it in my head. I had never met someone so selfish in my whole life.

It had been almost three months since I had first started to feel unwell. I had lost near a stone and a half in weight without even trying and although my new tablets had been working at first and I had started to get my appetite back, things then started going in reverse. My appetite was disappearing again and Mum and Mark were worried about me.

The appointment for my scopes into my bowels and stomach up at Perth Royal Infirmary eventually came through and I was nervous. I had not once taken a day off work since I fell ill. I had plodded through each day doing what I could, resting in between work to preserve my energy. On that day though I was taking the day off to go through and have my procedure done. Mark took the day off too as I didn't want to go alone.

I was sedated and they quickly did what they needed to do to get a better look at my digestive tract. It was all over so quick which was a relief as I had built up so much anxiety inside waiting on the appointment. The worst bit had been the day previous where I had to drink a solution to completely clear me out and wasn't allowed to eat for well over 24 hrs. I was absolutely starving by the time I was released from the hospital. Mark took me to a nice little place for a bar lunch and I scoffed it down, relieved that it was all over.

The results showed that my colon was slightly inflamed and that I had borderline Ibd, irritable bowel disease. Mark had also come to my specialist appointment through at Ninewells hospital and the doctor explained exactly what was happening to my body to not only myself but to Mark so that he would have a better understanding of what I was going through. He explained that what was happening to me was what the specialists called an extreme flare up and for me it had been the worst illness I had ever had, way worse than the horrible constant morning sickness I had had with all my pregnancies and worse than any stomach bug I had ever had. I was completely drained.

Although Mark had always been sympathetic of what I was going through it was a relief to me to have him truly know what was wrong with me. The best step forward then was to start taking a low dose of an anti depressant that would suppress the nerves in my bowels and it worked wonders. Within a couple of weeks of taking my new medication I was feeling so much better. I had energy again and was eating whole meals and more so I was enjoying my food again.

"Keep people in your life that truly love you, motivate you, encourage you, enhance you and make you feel happy."

It had been a couple of months since Nancy and I had fallen out and she had recently had her 30th birthday party which of course I wasn't at. I was starting to miss the company and the girly laughs. Nadine never bothered with me and Skylar had always been a busy person only occasionally making it to breakfasts which of course we weren't having anymore or at least I wasn't invited to. Tess was every now and again meeting up with me for a coffee and we never stopped speaking to one another online but at first she didn't like the rest of the girls knowing we were doing so which made it look like I was isolating myself from the rest of the group when I wasn't.

Before I had blocked Nancy's phone number, I had said to the girls that I would meet them for breakfast some morning when Nancy wasn't going and Nadine took it upon herself to twist my words and tell Nancy something that I hadn't said. My wording hadn't been nasty but Nadine at her best was trying to cause more hassle. Nancy took it upon herself to message me saying that under no circumstances was she going to be left out when we were meeting up. It wasn't what I had said or meant in my message I simply said that I would meet with them when Nancy wasn't there. She could have her time with the girls and I would have mine. Nadine of course took Nancy's side saying that she didn't have time to be having different catch ups. That I wasn't bothered about as I had had enough of her shit stirring, if she didn't want to meet me for breakfast that was her loss not mine.

It was Skylar's birthday and we had decided to meet for an evening meal at a local pub, just the two of us. There had been stuff going on at home and she needed someone to talk to. As soon as Nadine found out she was accusing me of all sorts behind my back. She cornered Skylar and said I was trying to cause a divide within the group, that we always did birthdays celebration together as a group. What was it going to take to get her to realise that there was no Wow group anymore? It was actually her that was causing the divide, she was the one shit stirring and it was only her that said she didn't have the time to keep up with both me and Nancy separately. She chose to be Nancy's side kick instead but it was no loss to me as I didn't have the time for her either. I had known for a very long time that she couldn't be trusted and the funny thing was that Nancy had told me she felt the exact same about her so when Nadine chose to take a side instead of playing it neutral like everyone else, I couldn't help but smile.

She was deluded if she thought I was going to sit around a table and eat with both her and Nancy during a birthday celebration and the thing was that Skylar invited me out that night not the other way round. People forgot that Skylar and I had been friends way longer than anyone else but although Nancy for a very long time had been my closest friend, what Nadine had done had in fact pushed Skylar and I closer together.

As time passed by and people started to realise that Nancy and I would never be friends again, life got easier and although the things that happened will never be forgiven or forgotten, my life sailed on in a happier mode. Tess continued to make an effort and still to this day we make time to catch up. Skylar, Skylar's husband Issac, Mark and I make an effort to have regular nights out either out for a meal and drinks in town or in each of our houses for the same.

The break-up of the little group we liked to call Wow was the best possible thing that could off happened for me. We had become a sort of clique and nobody was usually included in our nights out or meetings for breakfast and lunch. We had isolated other people from joining in and it wasn't healthy for anyone. I had wanted to have my cousin Charley and Kate join in on some of our girlie nights in but every time I mentioned it to Nancy it had been frowned upon. The weird thing looking back now was that on nights out it was always ok for her to have people tag along but she didn't like it if we wanted to include others. I had been so blinded by her that it's almost unbelievable that I had been so stupid.

Now I feel like a free spirit, I speak to whoever I wish. I can include whoever I wish and I don't feel suppressed by other people's negative energy. I am who I am and I'm proud to say I am me. The people who remain in my life mean the world to me and the old faces that have resurfaced from the cracks to say hello are my breath of fresh air.

"You can't start the next chapter of your life if you keep re-reading the last one...."

"Eventually all things fall into place. Until then, laugh at the confusion, live for the moment and know that everything happens for a reason....."   _Albert Schweitzer

Chapter Thirty Three

So much had happened in 2014, I had known it was going to be a busy one and an expensive one at the same time but I would never off guessed truly how much joy it would hold and at the same time how much it would cost me physically and emotionally. So far I had celebrated my Mums 50th, been on a hen party up to Inverness, helped celebrate the birthday of my best friends little one, been to see One Direction, watched my little cousin get married, fallen ill and lost my best friend. And it had all happened in a space of 7 months.

"Of all of the things that can be stolen from you – your possessions, your youth, your health, your words, your rights – what no one can ever take from you is your freedom to choose what you will believe in, and who and what your heart will love"

Dillan and Kate had been across for one of our usual nights of catching up with food and booze when we discovered that they had booked to go to Florida for a family holiday the following year, in 2015. We had previously discussed going on holiday together that year to celebrate Mark and Dillan's 40th birthdays but when I learnt they were going to American I was a little disappointed as I thought that our plans would now be out the window.

Kate explained that she desperately wanted us to come too but at first we thought there would be no way we could afford it. But after doing some sums and remembering that by the end of 2014 we would be out of our trust deed, meant that we would be up £300 a month, the holiday was actually going to be within our grasp should we be careful and save hard.

Dillan did some enquiring the next day to find out if we could get on the same flight as them and stay at the same hotel and it was all doable. All we needed to do was to raise the £300 deposit to secure the booking. We were all so happy when we finally got it booked and got the paper work through to confirm it all. I was finally going to conquer my fear of flying and I was going to get to go to Universal studios, which was where I had wanted to go since a small girl. Not only that but we booked tickets to go to Lego land, Jacks dream but in Florida and Seaworld which was Shannons dream, she desperately wanted to swim with the dolphins.

We decided to keep it a secret from the kids as we wanted to surprise them on Christmas morning with the news. I made up a sort of treasure hunt for them with clues to their big surprise on the day. We told them we had booked a holiday to Legoland Windsor that was costing a lot of money, that way they would start saving their pocket money. It was all very sneaky but for a good cause and I was bursting at the seams dying to tell them. Mark and I would sit up after the kids had gone to bed and watch videos on You Tube of all the attractions we would see and it was all becoming so real.

September 29th 2014 and Mark and I had kept the promise we had made to each other to go back to our honeymoon destination to celebrate our 10th wedding anniversary. It was so nice to be getting a break just the two of us. We had decided that we weren't going to fill our time away with quite as much outings as we had done on our honeymoon. We were going to make the most of it and relax, make the most of our surroundings and spent some quality time in our little romantic lodge complete with hot tub.

It was so nice to be back, the luxury was out of this world. There were chocolates, champagne and a lovely card sitting for us when we arrived along with relaxing music playing in the back ground. The towels were cleverly made into swans facing each over on top of the four poster bed, forming a love heart and to top it off it was a beautiful day outside meaning me were stripped off and in the hot tub before we had finished unpacking.

During the day we went for walks, visited nearby towns for shopping and chilled out in the hot tub or watched movies cuddled up on the sofa. At nights we were either in the hot tub or cuddled up in front of our log burning fire all nice and relaxed and loving our time away. Unfortunately there wasn't much in the way of sex. What we both needed at the time was to just enjoy each other's company and enjoy the relaxation. I wasn't at all bothered, I had put my body to hell and back the last few months and Mark had been really stressed out at work.

It was during one of our days out while having a bar lunch that Mark got another job offer from the same company and I truly believed that this time he was going to jump ship. I think in the end what made him turn it down was the quality time we were spending together. Deep down I didn't really want him to take a job where he would be away from home but I knew he needed it. He said he didn't want to miss out on life with us but also he was worried about money he would have to pay back to the company he worked for. They had paid to put him through some courses that he knew he would have to pay back should he ever resign and we didn't have the extra money. He used our remaining days away to think it over and just when I thought he was going to take it, he turned it down.

Days later he learned that they would off helped him out and paid him a wage up front to pay off the money he would owe. He phoned back to accept the job only to be told that they had already given it to someone else. He was gutted and I was upset to see him gutted at the missed opportunity. He never gave up though, the company knew who of him and of his work ethic and I know for certain that one day soon his time will come, I'm positive of that.

It was a week after the relaxation of our wee holiday when Mark and I finally got our libido back. We were all relaxed and now finally knew where we stood for now on the job front. We spent the weekend like sex crazed bunnies at it where and when we could, almost getting caught when Shannon's friend looked through the living room blinds when we didn't answer the front door. We saw her shadow and made a dive to the floor behind the couch. It was so funny and made the sex all the more fun. When the kids were home we locked them out of our bedroom and he fucked me on the bed as I screamed into the pillow with pleasure.

He said the most amazing thing to me that weekend. I had been joking about plastic surgery. He knew I would like a boob enhancement one day and he was all for it. I had joked about a tummy tuck and had said that I wished there was some sort of miracle procedure where they would take away all my tiger stripes. I didn't like my stretch marks from being pregnant but hadn't until then wished for them to be taken away. They were my war wounds and I was proud of them but really if I could get them taken away then up until that moment I would off. He told me that he would never want me to get rid of them. They were a permanent reminder for us both of the birth of our two amazing children that not only did I carry for him but we had made together.

In that moment I felt pure and utter love. He had been right there through everything. He had picked me up when I was down, wiped my tears when I cried, held me tight when I needed him close. We had shared laughter together but most of all he made me love life. He was the man of my dreams, my soul mate. He was my husband and my lover, he was not only a friend but he was my BEST FRIEND. I knew now where I belonged. It had been right there in front of my eyes all along. It was right here with my family.

" Two souls had touched one another like two sides of a heart combining as one. Wings would forever be wrapped around one another, cocooned with everlasting love. Their journey through life would be together filled with purpose and light. " *_Mary L Sibbit*

" Success comes in a lot of ways, but it doesn't come with money and it doesn't come with fame. It comes from having a meaning in your life, doing what you love and being passionate about what you do. That's having a life of success. When you have the ability to do what you love, love what you do and have the ability to impact people. That's having a life of success. That's what having a life of meaning is." _Tim Tebow

Epilogue

I had spent my whole life searching for my sense of belonging. As a child my life had been blown apart then as a teenager like others that age, I experimented and searched my soul for where to fit in. I grew tired and weary with life, had lost who I was, not knowing my purpose. Then my soul was touched in a way that I had not expected. My future husband when least expecting it walked into my life.

My life had been full of change, fluctuations and bouts of depression, anxiety, panic disorders and irritable bowel syndrome. Surroundings had changed, occupations had changed and friends had always come and gone. But the one stable thing that remained in my life, the one constant, was my family.

I was the richest person in the world. Not for the money and possessions that I had but because my life was filled with love. I had my husband, I had my children and I had my parents. I had finally realised where I belonged and it was right here, right now in the heart of my family. Being a mother and a wife was destined to bring me my inner happiness and finding my creative and spiritual side gave me a way to be at peace.

Postscript

One day a butterfly came to me. It landed right in front of my very eyes and no matter what I was doing or where I went, it followed me. Feeling uplifted and free from the negativity that had crossed my path I could see clearly again. My spiritual side had awoken. That one little butterfly meant so much. It became an inspiration to so many things in my life and even though I didn't know it at the time, it helped me to bring this book together. It opened my heart again to art and poetry, became my inspiration for not only a collection of art pieces but a series of poetry. I could feel its love and knew that loved ones that had passed were right there with me, by my side coaxing me forward to follow my dreams.

I peacefully drift though my life and take on all the challenges thrown my way with a clear head. My heart is full of love and my soul full of light. My life is fulfilled. I continue to enjoy my day job, running my cake business. In my spare time I take inspiration from my dreams and desires and throw them into my artwork and writing. I have been so lucky in life to have been given this gift, a gift that means that I can not only transform the images in my head into cakes and paintings but I can transform my feelings to writing by putting pen to paper.

I will never expect my life to be perfect and I truly believe that my dreams at night keep me grounded, but when things go wrong it does so to teach us something. Everyone has problems and everyone gets hurt at some point in their life, its learning how to deal with it and how to move forward that's the gift. Let go of the past and be the person you truly want to be.

Behind the cover

An open black mass of the emptiness, of the time yet to be.
A shimmer of light, the hope of what life beholds me.
White pebbles, all the things in life that have made me, me.
Layered and layered with varied edges to portray their meaning to me.
A solid pebble heart full of bright light, my family, my solidarity, my rock, my forever love. It strength lives on, it's what's strong for me.
A butterfly for the resurrection of things buried within me.
Red for the passion, for the love and for the lust..... please love thee?
Wings spread wide baring my soul for all to see.
Transformed from the darkness, metamorphosed in life through a love deep within me.
A soft shadow as I cast my wings to take flight. But maybe......
I could fly. But my family ground me. x

In Loving memory of my family who no longer walk with us.

May you continue to sparkle in the sky brightening our nights.

Until we meet again..... x

DID1856985

#0037 - 020617 - C0 - 210/148/16 - PB - DID1856985